PSALMS

EXODUS AND LEVITICUS SECTIONS
Psalms 42—89

J. Vernon McGee

THOMAS NELSON PUBLISHERS

Nashville

Published in Nashville, Tennessee, by Thomas Nelson, Inc.

Quotations from *The Numerical Bible: Psalms* by F. W. Grant are used by permission of the publisher, Loizeaux Brothers, Inc., Neptune, New Jersey.

Excerpts from *The Book of Psalms* by Arno C. Gaebelein are used by permission of the publishers, Loizeaux Brothers, Inc., Neptune, New Jersey.

Excerpts from *The New Scofield Reference Bible, King James Version,* copyright © 1967 by Oxford University Press, Inc., are reprinted by permission.

Scripture quotations are from the KING JAMES VERSION of the Bible.

Library of Congress Cataloging-in-Publication Data

McGee, J. Vernon (John Vernon), 1904–1988
   [Thru the Bible with J. Vernon McGee]
   Thru the Bible commentary series / J. Vernon McGee.
     p.   cm.
   Reprint. Originally published: Thru the Bible with J. Vernon McGee. 1975.
   Includes bibliographical references.
   ISBN 0-8407-3269-4
   1. Bible—Commentaries. I. Title.
BS491.2.M37 1991
220.7′7—dc20
                                  90–41340
                                       CIP

Printed in the United States of America
2 3 4 5 6 7 — 96 95 94 93

CONTENTS

PSALMS 42—89

PREFACE

The radio broadcasts of the Thru the Bible Radio five-year program were transcribed, edited, and published first in single-volume paperbacks to accommodate the radio audience.

There has been a minimal amount of further editing for this publication. Therefore, these messages are not the word-for-word recording of the taped messages which went out over the air. The changes were necessary to accommodate a reading audience rather than a listening audience.

These are popular messages, prepared originally for a radio audience. They should not be considered a commentary on the entire Bible in any sense of that term. These messages are devoid of any attempt to present a theological or technical commentary on the Bible. Behind these messages is a great deal of research and study in order to interpret the Bible from a popular rather than from a scholarly (and too-often boring) viewpoint.

We have definitely and deliberately attempted "to put the cookies on the bottom shelf so that the kiddies could get them."

The fact that these messages have been translated into many languages for radio broadcasting and have been received with enthusiasm reveals the need for a simple teaching of the whole Bible for the masses of the world.

I am indebted to many people and to many sources for bringing this volume into existence. I should express my especial thanks to my secretary, Gertrude Cutler, who supervised the editorial work; to Dr. Elliott R. Cole, my associate, who handled all the detailed work with the publishers; and finally, to my wife Ruth for tenaciously encouraging me from the beginning to put my notes and messages into printed form.

Solomon wrote, ". . . of making many books there is no end; and much study is a weariness of the flesh" (Eccl. 12:12). On a sea of books that flood the marketplace, we launch this series of THRU THE BIBLE with the hope that it might draw many to the one Book, *The Bible*.

J. VERNON McGEE

The Book of

PSALMS

INTRODUCTION

The title in the Hebrew means *Praises* or *Book of Praises*. The title in the Greek suggests the idea of an instrumental accompaniment. Our title comes from the Greek *psalmos*. It is the book of worship. It is the hymn book of the temple.

Many writers contributed one or more psalms. David, "the sweet psalmist of Israel," has seventy-three psalms assigned to him. (Psalm 2 is ascribed to him in Acts 4:25; Psalm 95 is ascribed to him in Hebrews 4:7.) Also he could be the author of some of the "orphanic" psalms. He was peculiarly endowed to write these songs from experience as well as by a special aptitude. He arranged those in existence in his day for temple use. The other writers are as follows: Moses, 1 (90th); Solomon, 2; Sons of Korah, 11; Asaph, 12; Heman, 1 (88th); Ethan, 1 (89th); Hezekiah, 10; "orphanic," 39 (David may be the writer of some of these). There are 150 psalms.

Christ (the Messiah) is prominent throughout. The King and the kingdom are the theme songs of the Psalms.

The key word in the Book of Psalms is *hallelujah*, that is, *praise the Lord*. This phrase has become a Christian cliché, but it is one that should cause a swelling of great emotion in the soul. Hallelujah, praise the Lord!

Psalms 50 and 150 I consider to be the key psalms. Psalm 50, a psalm of Asaph, probably tells more than any other. Psalm 150 is the hallelujah chorus—the word *hallelujah* occurs thirteen times in its six brief verses. It concludes the Book of Psalms and could be considered the chorus of all other psalms.

The Psalms record deep devotion, intense feeling, exalted emotion, and dark dejection. They play upon the keyboard of the human soul with all the stops pulled out. Very candidly, I feel overwhelmed when I come to this marvelous book. It is located in the very center of God's Word. Psalm 119 is in the very center of the Word of God, and it exalts His Word.

This book has blessed the hearts of multitudes down through the ages. When I have been sick at home, or in the hospital, or when some problem is pressing upon my mind and heart, I find myself always turning to the Psalms. They always bless my heart and life. Apparently down through the ages it has been that way. Ambrose, one of the great saints of the church, said, "The Psalms are the voices of the church." Augustine said, "They are the epitome of the whole Scripture." Martin Luther said, "They are a little book for all saints." John Calvin said, "They are the anatomy of all parts of the soul." I like that.

Someone has said that there are 126 psychological experiences—I don't know how they arrived at that number—but I do know that all of them are recorded in the Book of Psalms. It is the *only* book which contains every experience of a human being. The Psalms run the psychological gamut. Every thought, every impulse, every emotion that sweeps over the soul is recorded in this book. That is the reason, I suppose, that it always speaks to our hearts and finds a responsive chord wherever we turn.

Hooker said of the Psalms, "They are the choice and flower of all things profitable in other books." Donne put it this way, "The Psalms foretell what I, what any, shall do and suffer and say." Herd called the Psalms, "A hymnbook for all time." Watts said, "They are the thousand-voiced heart of the church." The place Psalms have held in the lives of God's people testifies to their universality, although they have a peculiar Jewish application. They express the deep feelings of all believing hearts in all generations.

The Psalms are full of Christ. There is a more complete picture of Him in the Psalms than in the Gospels. The Gospels tell us that He went to the mountain to pray, but the Psalms give us His prayer. The Gospels tell us that He was crucified, but the Psalms tell us what went on in His own heart during the Crucifixion. The Gospels tell us He went back to heaven, but the Psalms begin where the Gospels leave off and show us Christ seated in heaven.

Christ the Messiah is prominent throughout this book. You will remember that the Lord Jesus, when He appeared after His resurrection to those who were His own, said to them, ". . . These are the words which I spake unto you, while I was yet with you, that all things must be fulfilled, which were written in the law of Moses, and in the prophets, and in the psalms, concerning me" (Luke 24:44). Christ is the subject of the Psalms. I think He is the object of praise in every one of them. I will not be able to locate Him in every one of them, but that does not mean that He is not in each psalm; it only means that Vernon McGee is limited. Although all of them have Christ as the object of worship, some are technically called messianic psalms. These record the birth, life, death, resurrection, glory, priesthood, kingship, and return of Christ. There are sixteen messianic psalms that speak specifically about Christ, but as I have already said, all 150 of them are about Him. The Book of Psalms is a hymnbook and a HIM book—it is all about Him. As we study it, that fact will become very clear.

In a more restrictive sense, the Psalms deal with Christ belonging to Israel and Israel belonging to Christ. Both themes are connected to the rebellion of man. There is no blessing on this earth until Israel and Christ are brought together. The Psalms are Jewish in expectation and hope. They are songs which were adapted to temple worship. That does not mean, however, that they do not have a spiritual application and interpretation for us today. They certainly do. I probably turn to them more than to any other portion of the Word of God, but we need to be a little more exacting in our interpretation of the Psalms. For example, God is not spoken of as a Father in this book. The saints are not called sons. In the Psalms He is God the Father, not the Father God. The abiding presence of the Holy Spirit and the blessed hope of the New Testament are not in this book. Failure to recognize this has led many people astray in their interpretation of Psalm 2. The reference in this song is not to the rapture of the church but to the second coming of Christ to the earth to establish His kingdom and to reign in Jerusalem.

The imprecatory psalms have caused the most criticism because of their vindictiveness and prayers for judgment. These psalms came from a time of war and from a people who under law were looking for justice and peace on earth. My friend, you cannot have peace without putting down unrighteousness and rebellion. Apparently God intends to do just that, and He makes no apology for it. In His own time He will move in judgment upon this earth. In the New Testament the Christian is told to love his enemies, and it may startle you to read prayers in the Psalms that say some very harsh things about the enemy. But judgment is to bring justice upon this earth. Also there are psalms that anticipate the period when Antichrist will be in power. We have no reasonable basis to dictate how people should act or what they should pray under such circumstances.

Other types of psalms include the penitential, historic, nature, pilgrim, Hallel, missionary, puritan, acrostic, and praise of God's Word. This is a rich section we are coming to. We are going to mine for gold and diamonds here, my friend.

The Book of Psalms is not arranged in a haphazard sort of way. Some folk seem to think that the Psalms were dropped into a tub, shaken up, then put together with no arrangement. However, it is interesting to note that one psalm will state a principle, then there will follow several psalms that will be explanatory. Psalms 1—8 are an example of this.

The Book of Psalms is arranged in an orderly manner. In fact, it has been noted for years that the Book of Psalms is arranged and corresponds to the Pentateuch of Moses. There are Genesis, Exodus, Leviticus, Numbers, and Deuteronomy sections, as you will see in the outline which follows.

The correspondence between the Psalms and the Pentateuch is easily seen. For instance, in the Genesis section you see the perfect man in a state of blessedness, as in Psalm 1. Next you have the fall and recovery of man in view. Psalm 2 pictures the rebellious man. In

Psalm 3 is the perfect man rejected. In Psalm 4 we see the conflict between the seed of the woman and the serpent. In Psalm 5 we find the perfect man in the midst of enemies. Psalm 6 presents the perfect man in the midst of chastisement with the bruising of his heel. In Psalm 7 we see the perfect man in the midst of false witnesses. Finally, in Psalm 8 we see the salvation of man coming through the bruising of the head. In Psalms 9—15 we see the enemy and Antichrist conflict and the final deliverance. Then in Psalms 16—41 we see Christ in the midst of His people sanctifying them to God. All of this will be seen as we go through the Book of Psalms.

Spurgeon said, "The Book of Psalms instructs us in the use of wings as well as words. It sets us both mounting and singing." This is the book that may make a skylark out of you instead of some other kind of a bird. This book has been called the epitome and analogy of the soul. It has also been designated as the garden of the Scriptures. Out of 219 quotations of the Old Testament in the New Testament, 116 of them are from the Psalms. You will see 150 spiritual songs which undoubtedly at one time were all set to music. This is a book which ought to make our hearts sing.

OUTLINE

I. Genesis Section, Psalms 1—41
Man seen in a state of blessedness, fall, and recovery (Man in View)
- A. Perfect Man (Last Adam), Psalm 1
- B. Rebellious Man, Psalm 2
- C. Perfect Man Rejected, Psalm 3
- D. Conflict between Seed of Woman and Serpent, Psalm 4
- E. Perfect Man in Midst of Enemies, Psalm 5
- F. Perfect Man in Midst of Chastisement (Bruising Heel), Psalm 6
- G. Perfect Man in Midst of False Witnesses, Psalm 7
- H. Repair of Man Comes through Man (Bruising Head), Psalm 8
- I. Enemy and Antichrist Conflict; Final Deliverance, Psalms 9—15
- J. Christ in Midst of His People Sanctifying Them to God, Psalms 16—41

II. Exodus Section, Psalms 42—72
Ruin and Redemption (Israel in View)
- A. Israel's Ruin, Psalms 42—49
- B. Israel's Redeemer, Psalms 50—60
- C. Israel's Redemption, Psalms 61—72

III. Leviticus Section, Psalms 73—89
Darkness and dawn (Sanctuary in View)
Tabernacle, temple, house, assembly and congregation in almost every psalm.

IV. Numbers Section, Psalms 90—106
Peril and protection (Earth in View)

V. Deuteronomy Section, Psalms 107—150
Perfection and praise of the Word of God

EXODUS SECTION

Ruin and Redemption (Israel in view)
Psalms 42—72

Psalms 42—72 comprise the Exodus section. As in the Book of Exodus, we will see God's people in a strange land, a suffering people away from the Land of Promise. The heel of a dictator is on them. You hear them groan and moan, and you hear the whip of the taskmaster falling upon them. They are in great trouble, which increases rather than decreases. Finally Israel's cries and groans are heard, and the Lord arises on behalf of His suffering people. He makes good His covenant to Abraham, Isaac, and Jacob. Then the Lord delivers them out of the land of Egypt. For example, in the first seven psalms (42—48) we find conditions as they were at the beginning of the Book of Exodus. But these psalms do not refer to the past; they look to the future and reveal the experiences of the remnant of Israel in the days that lie ahead. We will see God's chosen people away from Jerusalem; they are separated from the holy place and out of touch with Jehovah, just as they were in Egypt.

In the Genesis and Exodus sections of the Psalms there is an interesting contrast of the names of God. In the Genesis section the name *Jehovah* occurs 272 times, while the name *Elohim* occurs only fifteen times. In the Exodus section the name *Elohim* occurs 164 times, and the name *Jehovah* occurs only thirty times. What is the significance of this? These two personal names of God have different meanings. Elohim speaks of the fullness of God's divine power. The name *Jehovah* is involved in redemption. Jehovah is the One who keeps Israel.

We will find that David did not write as many of the psalms in this section as he did in the last one. David wrote nineteen of the psalms, and seven of them were written by the sons of Korah who were connected with the Levitical family. All of the psalms in this division are a prophetic picture of Israel in the last days.

In Psalms 42—44 we see the children of Israel in Egypt with Pharaoh ruling over them. Psalm 43 mentions the Antichrist, and Israel is mourning because of the oppression of the enemy. We find them crying out to God to deliver them, and deliverance comes to them. Psalm 45 is the great millennial psalm which speaks of the Lord Jesus coming to reign on the earth.

Something important for God's people to see is that the primary and fundamental interpretation of these psalms is applicable to the nation of Israel. They look to the future during the time of trouble called the Great Tribulation. Therefore, we need to be careful when we lift out a verse from one of the psalms to ask the question, "How does it really apply to us?" We can apply many of the psalms to our needs today. God's children, who are in trouble, can find real solace and comfort in them, but we must never forget that their primary application is to Israel. I think it is a terrible thing to exclude Israel from the plan and purpose of God for the future as many people do. It is almost like writing off a certain portion of God's Word, and saying, "Yes, I believe in the inspiration of Scripture that applies to me, but if it supposedly applies to other people that I am not concerned about, it is not the Word of God." There is danger today in that type of thinking.

Let us keep in mind that when the psalmist speaks of Israel he is not referring to the whole nation of Israel, for the entire nation is not in view. We see this distinction also in the word *church*. Is the church made up of all the names of people on membership rolls in every church regardless of the denomination? I don't think so. The church is made up of a body of believers who have trusted the Lord Jesus Christ as Savior. You don't become a member of the true church by joining a visible church and having your name put on a church roll or by going through a ceremony of some kind. Only a personal relationship with Christ can make you a member of the true church. We should always make a distinction between the organized church and what is generally called the *invisible* church. The remnant of the nation of Israel is not the entire nation, just as all members of the organized church do not make up the invisible church, or body of believers. It is the believing remnant of Israel that we will be looking at in this Exodus section of the Book of Psalms.

PSALMS 42 AND 43

THEME: *Heart cry of the God-fearing remnant*

This psalm presents the future suffering of the godly remnant of Israel during the Great Tribulation period. When Israel was in the land of Egypt (Exod. 12), God first redeemed them by blood. The blood of the Passover lamb was sprinkled on the doorposts of the houses by those who believed God. At night the death angel passed over the homes, and if blood was there no one died. This was redemption by *blood*. The second phase of redemption was at the Red Sea, and there it was redemption by *power*.

The inscription of this psalm is "Maschil, for the sons of Korah." *Maschil* means that it is a psalm of teaching, a psalm of understanding. You may recall that Korah led a rebellion during the period of Israel's wandering in the wilderness. God executed him because of his rebellion against the authority of Moses and Aaron, but his sons were spared. God made it very clear (Num. 26:9–11) that his sons did not die in God's judgment, but they continued their service before God. They are the ones who wrote these first few psalms of the Exodus section, which is quite wonderful.

Prophetically, this gives us a picture of the Great Tribulation period.

> **As the hart panteth after the water brooks, so panteth my soul after thee, O God.**
>
> **My soul thirsteth for God, for the living God: when shall I come and appear before God? [Ps. 42:1–2].**

Rather than going back to Egypt, I want to apply this to the future because there will be a time when these people, the Israelites, will be out of their land again. There are several excellent Bible expositors who believe that the present regathering of Jews in the land of Israel may eventuate in their dispersion again—that they will be put out of the land—perhaps in our day. The godly remnant is not in the land today. There are two groups in the land of Israel right now: one group we call the orthodox Jews who are waiting for their Messiah, expecting Him to come and wanting to rebuild the temple. The other group is not concerned with religious matters. They contend that a new era has begun. They have Egypt, the Arabs, and the United Nations to deal with.

The godly remnant of Israel, God's people, have a longing for God, as do God's people of all ages. They picture David. I think David could easily have said these words hiding in a cave overlooking a valley. He could have heard hunters and the barking of the dogs and, in a few minutes, a rustle in the bushes. David's men on guard duty became alert. There is a little spring near the opening of the cave, and soon a little deer, foaming at the mouth, his sides lathered, plunges his head into the water and takes a good deep drink. He waits a moment, listening, then he takes another drink.

Therefore the psalmist could say, "As the hart panteth after the water brooks, so panteth my soul after thee, O God." Is that the way you feel about God? There are those who claim that if you become very legalistic and keep the Ten Commandments you are pleasing to God. My friend, man is alienated from God; he needs more than the Ten Commandments. The Ten Commandments show us that we are sinners, and we are in rebellion against God. We have no desire or capacity for Him. We need, therefore, to be born again. We need to be brought into the family of God and to the place where we can say, not just as a verse in Scripture but from our hearts, "As the hart panteth after the water brooks, so panteth my soul after thee, O God."

This will be especially meaningful to the remnant of Israel, but it is meaningful right now to many of God's children.

My tears have been my meat day and night, while they continually say unto me, Where is thy God? [Ps. 42:3].

There was much weeping in the brickyards of Egypt and will be in the future. This will be the taunt during the Great Tribulation period: "Where is your God? When is Messiah coming?"

> **Why art thou cast down, O my soul? and why art thou disquieted in me? hope thou in God: for I shall yet praise him for the help of his countenance [Ps. 42:5].**

He rebukes himself for his despondency and encourages himself to trust in God.

> **O my God, my soul is cast down within me: therefore will I remember thee from the land of Jordan, and of the Hermonites, from the hill Mizar.**
>
> **Deep calleth unto deep at the noise of thy waterspouts: all thy waves and thy billows are gone over me [Ps. 42:6-7].**

This is the language Jonah used in his prayer. "For thou hadst cast me into the deep, in the midst of the seas; and the floods compassed me about: all thy billows and thy waves passed over me" (Jonah 2:3). Jonah went down into the jaws of death. During the Great Tribulation Israel will think that destruction is upon them, but God will deliver them.

> **Yet the LORD will command his lovingkindness in the daytime, and in the night his song shall be with me, and my prayer unto the God of my life.**
>
> **I will say unto God my rock, Why hast thou forgotten me? why go I mourning because of the oppression of the enemy? [Ps. 42:8-9].**

Do you feel like that sometimes? I am sure that many of us do.

> **Why art thou cast down, O my soul? and why art thou disquieted within me? hope thou in God: for I shall yet praise him, who is the health of my countenance, and my God [Ps. 42:11].**

In his desperate hour he turns to God. In their desperate hours the remnant will turn to God. There will be no help from the east, the west, the north, or the south. My help comes from the Lord, the maker of heaven and earth.

Psalm 43 is closely connected with Psalm 42. The godly remnant calls on God to act in their behalf.

> **Judge me, O God, and plead my cause against an ungodly nation: O deliver me from the deceitful and unjust man [Ps. 43:1].**

This is the remnant of Israel speaking. The Antichrist is a liar. He will make a covenant with these people and then will break it in the midst of the "week." When this happens, their cry will be, "Deliver me from the deceitful and unjust man." I don't know if you have ever prayed this prayer or not, but I have said, "O God, don't let the dictator arise in the United States." There is grave danger of that. We need to ask Christ to deliver us from deceitful and unjust men. I certainly don't want him ruling over me, and we have had quite a few like that in our history. I am afraid the condition of our nation is due to the leadership and internal problems.

> **O send out thy light and thy truth: let them lead me; let them bring me unto thy holy hill, and to thy tabernacles [Ps. 43:3].**

"Send out thy light and thy truth." What is the psalmist praying for? Jesus said, ". . . I am the light of the world: he that followeth me shall not walk in darkness, but shall have the light of life" (John 8:12). He also said, ". . . I am the way, the truth, and the life: no man cometh unto the Father, but by me" (John 14:6). These statements of the Lord Jesus Christ were not lost on His hearers, because if they knew He was the light and the truth, they would also know He was the Messiah who had come to deliver them. "Let them bring me unto thy holy hill, and to thy tabernacles." He wants to go back to Jerusalem. He wants to worship in the temple and to be brought back to God.

> **Why art thou cast down, O my soul? and why art thou
> disquieted within me? hope in God: for I shall yet praise
> him, who is the health of my countenance, and my God
> [Ps. 43:5].**

Their prayers will be answered, and their long expected Messiah will return. At that time Ezekiel's prophecy will be fulfilled: "A new heart also will I give you, and a new spirit will I put within you: and I will take away the stony heart out of your flesh, and I will give you an heart of flesh. And I will put my spirit within you, and cause you to walk in my statutes, and ye shall keep my judgments, and do them. And ye shall dwell in the land that I gave to your fathers; and ye shall be my people, and I will be your God" (Ezek. 36:26–28).

PSALM 44

W e come now to another maschil psalm, a psalm of instruction, and it is from the sons of Korah.

Although it is impossible to determine the historical condition in Israel that called forth this prayer, we do know the prophetic interpretation. This will be the final experience of the faithful remnant of Israel before their Messiah returns to deliver them.

> **We have heard with our ears, O God, our fathers have told us, what work thou didst in their days, in the times of old [Ps. 44:1].**

Gideon said the same thing. "And Gideon said unto him, Oh my Lord, if the LORD be with us, why then is all this befallen us? and where be all his miracles which our fathers told us of, saying, Did not the LORD bring us up from Egypt? but now the LORD hath forsaken us, and delivered us into the hands of the Midianites" (Judg. 6:13). In that day of trouble, just when God is on the verge of delivering them again, Israel will refer to God's help in the past. God has intruded in history before, and He will do it again.

> **How thou didst drive out the heathen with thy hand, and plantedst them; how thou didst afflict the people, and cast them out [Ps. 44:2].**

This refers to the time of Moses and Joshua. God evicted the inhabitants of Canaan because of their gross sin and planted His chosen people there.

> **For they got not the land in possession by their own sword, neither did their own arm save them: but thy**

**right hand, and thine arm, and the light of thy counte-
nance, because thou hadst a favour unto them [Ps. 44:3].**

It was God who gave the land to the children of Israel. They did not
capture it because of their own strength or cleverness.

For our personal application, "Thy right hand" is the mighty bared
arm of God in salvation, revealed nineteen hundred years ago at the
cross.

Then listen to his heart cry that comes from him:

> **Thou art my King, O God: command deliverances for
> Jacob [Ps. 44:4].**

I hope you understand that "Jacob" is the man Jacob, and Jacob became the nation of Israel. When he cries, "Thou art my King, O God,"
he is talking about Israel's King. Our Lord Jesus is Israel's King, and
He will return to deliver His suffering people. Of course there is application for us, but let's keep the psalms in correct perspective so that
they will be more meaningful to us.

> **Through thee will we push down our enemies, through
> thy name will we tread them under that rise up against
> us.**

> **For I will not trust in my bow, neither shall my sword
> save me [Ps. 44:5–6].**

In that day of tribulation the godly remnant is going to ask for revenge.
They will be under Law, and they will have a right to do that.

Today we are to *pray* for those who deceitfully use us; we are told
even to *love* our enemies. That is a very difficult thing to do, but we
can turn our enemies over to the Lord. We are not to avenge ourselves
because the Lord says, ". . . Vengeance is mine; I will repay . . ." (Rom.
12:19). There are many people we should turn over to the Lord, not
only for salvation, but for reasons of vengeance. I am not talking about
people who have caused us some personal grievance, but those who
are trying to hinder the giving out of the Word of God. It is a terrible

thing to try to blacken the name of a man or woman who stands for the things of God. You should be careful before you criticize your pastor. Make sure your facts are true. To some people a pastor represents God's cause on earth. They will judge God largely by what he says. If you discredit him, you discredit God in their eyes. I think this is why many young people have turned away from the Bible and the church. Many of them have grown up in Christian homes, and their parents have served "roast preacher" each Sunday. It is wrong to discredit a man who is giving out the Word of God. If things seem to be wrong, we should ask God to intervene rather than to try to take matters into our own hands.

Israel is in deep trouble. The enemy is raging against them; that "little horn" that Daniel mentioned ". . . shall wear out the saints of the Most High . . ." (Dan. 7:25). These are Jewish saints, and Antichrist makes war against them to overcome them. They are warned not to fight back. They refuse the mark of the beast, and they are killed in large numbers. In their distress they cry out to God. I think this will be the darkest moment in the history of the world.

> **Yea, for thy sake are we killed all the day long; we are counted as sheep for the slaughter [Ps. 44:22].**

This verse is not a picture of the church right now, would you say? There are many believers suffering for Christ's sake; but by and large, the church is not under persecution. However, the remnant of Israel will be persecuted; and it is the remnant that is in view here. I want to keep that clear.

> **Awake, why sleepest thou, O Lord? arise, cast us not off for ever [Ps. 44:23].**

Here is a cry for God to wake up. Well, God is not asleep. It is in their desperation that the remnant cries out. During the time of the Maccabees, between the Old and New Testaments, the enemies of Israel came to the foreground. As far as the past is concerned, it was the time that Israel suffered more than at any other time in their history; but it will be nothing compared to the suffering they will endure during the Great Tribulation period. During the Maccabean period there was a group of priests called the "wakers." They were the ones who cried out to God saying, "Awake, why sleepest thou, O Lord?" During this time people felt like God was asleep. But John Hyrcanus, one of the great Maccabees, a high priest, put an end to this practice. He asked the people, "Does the Deity sleep? Hath not the Scripture said, 'Behold, the keeper of Israel slumbereth and sleepeth not?'" You don't have to ask God to wake up even though there are times when you feel like it. In that future day the remnant will feel that He is asleep and say, "Awake, why sleepest thou, O Lord?" When that day comes, God will not be asleep. He will be ready to move. He will not cast off His people forever.

> **Wherefore hidest thou thy face, and forgettest our affliction and our oppression?**
>
> **For our soul is bowed down to the dust: our belly cleaveth unto the earth.**
>
> **Arise for our help, and redeem us for thy mercies' sake [Ps. 44:24–26].**

From the darkest moment in the history of this world comes a cry from the remnant for God to redeem them for His mercies' sake. This is a plea for help and justice.

PSALM 45

THEME: *The coming of Christ to establish His kingdom on this earth*

This is a messianic psalm and is so quoted in the Epistle to the Hebrews. This is another maschil psalm, that is, for instruction, written by the sons of Korah, and is inscribed "To the chief Musician upon Shoshannim," which means "lilies." It is a picture of Christ as the Messiah—He is the Lily of the Valley as well as the Rose of Sharon. In translating this, the Targumim adds, "Thy beauty, O King Messiah, is greater than that of the children of men."

This very wonderful psalm speaks of the second coming of Christ. This changes the tenor of the Psalms from the cry of a people in the anguish of tribulation to the glorious triumph of their coming King, as it is described in Revelation, chapter 19. Our Lord Jesus Christ spoke of it also (Matt. 24:29–30), and it is the hope of the world.

My heart is inditing a good matter: I speak of the things which I have made touching the king: my tongue is the pen of a ready writer [Ps. 45:1].

"My heart is inditing" means bursting forth or overflowing. There is something he must say and wishes he could tell it, because his tongue moves faster than his pen. That is true of many of us. Have you ever been excited about something and have tried to put it in a letter to a friend, and when you read it over you see how inadequate it is and wish you could tell it instead of write it? I had that experience a few minutes ago—I couldn't say what I wanted to say to a friend in a letter; so I called him by phone. Well, the psalmist couldn't call us by telephone, so we have Psalm 45 in printed form.

MESSIAH, HIS PERSON AND POWER

Thou art fairer than the children of men: grace is poured into thy lips: therefore God hath blessed thee for ever [Ps. 45:2].

This is a lovely psalm which is occupied with the person of Christ. Paul mentioned that: "But we all, with open face beholding as in a glass the glory of the Lord, are changed into the same image from glory to glory, even as by the Spirit of the Lord" (2 Cor. 3:18). My friend, we need to behold Him more.

In this psalm we are seeing Him, not as a Savior, but as a King.

Gird thy sword upon thy thigh, O most mighty, with thy glory and thy majesty [Ps. 45:3].

This is a picture of Christ coming forward, not as Savior, but as the King at His second coming. Israel expected Messiah to come to earth with a sword. The first time He came to earth He came without a sword. You will recall that when Jesus was arrested, one of His disciples drew his sword and cut off the ear of the servant of the high priest. And Jesus said, ". . . Put up again thy sword into his place: for all they that take the sword shall perish with the sword" (Matt. 26:52). In our day they are looking for the Messiah who will bring peace, without a sword, but Psalm 2:9 says of the Lord, "Thou shalt break them with a rod of iron; thou shalt dash them in pieces like a potter's vessel." Psalm 2 speaks of Christ's coming to earth the second time. In fact, it is quoted several times in the Book of Revelation in respect to His second coming. When He returns, He is going to find the world in rebellion. The Antichrist will be in power. He will be persecuting God's people, both the remnant of Israel and that great company of Gentiles who turned to God.

"Grace is poured into his lips"—that is emphasized, but there will also be condemnation and judgment. I think we ought to be realistic, not idealistic. He will have to come in power and wrath against a world that is in rebellion against Him.

And in thy majesty ride prosperously because of truth and meekness and righteousness; and thy right hand shall teach thee terrible things [Ps. 45:4].

"Terrible things" means *awe-inspiring* things.

Notice, the Lord is riding to victory, and here are the three planks of His platform: truth, meekness, and righteousness. Do you know of any candidate today who uses these three planks in his platform? The candidates don't sound meek to me, and I wonder about the truth of their statements, and righteousness—well, the whole motive is to get elected, not to do right. How this poor nation needs a candidate who will speak truth, who exhibits a little meekness, and who goes all-out for righteousness. These are eternal principles of our Lord's kingdom. No president, leader, dictator, or king has ever come to power on this platform in the history of this world. This King is different. The character of Christ is truth; His words are truth—yet men call Him a liar. But all men are liars, not Christ. You won't hear the truth today in the halls of Congress, or in the marts of trade, or on Wall Street, or in our industrial complexes, or on our college campuses, or read it in the newspaper, or hear it on TV or radio—because all news is slanted. Unfortunately you can't even hear the truth in many of our churches. But our Lord is coming to power on the platform of truth and humility. Someone has said, "If you wish to astonish the whole world, tell the truth." That is the way our Lord is coming to power—it will be startling.

Thine arrows are sharp in the heart of the king's enemies; whereby the people fall under thee [Ps. 45:5].

This is a portrait of the King coming to earth.

MESSIAH, HIS GOVERNMENT AND GLORY

This is coronation day, and it is the key of this psalm.

Thy throne, O God, is for ever and ever: the sceptre of thy kingdom is a right sceptre [Ps. 45:6].

He is going to rule in righteousness. How the world needs a righteous ruler! Regarding His return to the earth, the Lord Jesus Himself said, "When the Son of man shall come in his glory, and all the holy angels with him, then shall he sit upon the throne of his glory" (Matt. 25:31). Not until then will we have peace on this earth. That is the need of the world. When Betsy Ross made the first American flag, George Washington expressed the wish that it would wave for a thousand years. We have recently celebrated our two hundredth anniversary, and already we are growing old as a nation. But the government of God is eternal.

Thou lovest righteousness, and hatest wickedness: therefore God, thy God, hath anointed thee with the oil of gladness above thy fellows [Ps. 45:7].

The Anointed One is Messiah, of which Christ is the Greek form. It is not a name, but it is His official title. The first time He came, He came as Prophet—the messenger and message of God—which refers to the past. In our day He is our Great High Priest at the right hand of God; that is His present ministry. But His second coming will be as King, the Messiah. This is for the future.

"God hath anointed thee with the oil of gladness." It is unfortunate that we tend to think of Him as a Man of Sorrows. I believe that He was the most joyous person on this earth when He was here.

That this is a messianic psalm referring to our Lord Jesus Christ is fully attested by the quotation of these two verses in the Epistle to the Hebrews: "But unto the Son he saith, Thy throne, O God, is for ever and ever: a sceptre of righteousness is the sceptre of thy kingdom. Thou hast loved righteousness, and hated iniquity; therefore God, even thy God, hath anointed thee with the oil of gladness above thy fellows" (Heb. 1:8–9). The critic who attempts to apply this psalm to Solomon or some unknown king fails to note that He is addressed as God. It is not conceivable that Solomon or any other king would be addressed as God. The entire first chapter of Hebrews presents our Lord Jesus in His exaltation, being the express image of God, far superior to angels, and seated at God's right hand.

**All thy garments smell of myrrh, and aloes, and cassia,
out of the ivory palaces, whereby they have made thee
glad [Ps. 45:8].**

He came to this earth that our joy might be full. And it was for "the joy
that was set before him" that He endured the cross. Oh, how we as
believers need to rejoice! The tribe of Judah, which means "praise,"
led the children of Israel in the wilderness march; yet they com-
plained, they whined, they sang the desert blues when they should
have been praising God. This is the same thing the church is doing in
our day. My friend, believers should be praising God—not complain-
ing! At Christmastime we sing the song, "Joy to the world! the Lord is
come; Let earth receive her King." That is not a Christmas hymn at all;
it refers to Christ's second coming and should not be relegated to a
seasonal section of our hymnbook.

Moving down in this wonderful psalm, we have a scene at court:

**Kings' daughters were among thy honourable women:
upon thy right hand did stand the queen in gold of
Ophir [Ps. 45:9].**

The church is not mentioned by name in the Old Testament, but I
believe you see it in type or in figures of speech. I think most of
the brides in the Old Testament are pictures of Christ and His bride,
the church. Examples of this are Eve, Rebekah, and Ruth. Who is the
queen in this verse? I believe she is a picture of the church, although
she is not specifically identified, and Christ will lift her to the throne.

**Hearken, O daughter, and consider, and incline thine
ear; forget also thine own people, and thy father's house
[Ps. 45:10].**

We are to leave the world. We are not to love the world. We have been
saved out of it. We are to cling to the Lord.

> **So shall the king greatly desire thy beauty: for he is thy
> Lord; and worship thou him [Ps. 45:11].**

The church is to be made beautiful. All sin will be removed. What a
prospect this is!

> **I will make thy name to be remembered in all genera-
> tions: therefore shall the people praise thee for ever and
> ever [Ps. 45:17].**

This verse speaks of the millennial kingdom. But the kingdom goes
on into eternity after the Lord has made a few adjustments, which
includes Satan being loosed for a time and then his being cast into the
lake of fire and brimstone. This is a glorious psalm, and when it is put
in proper perspective, it has great meaning for us today.

PSALM 46

THEME: God is our refuge, a song of the Millennium

The next three psalms form a little cluster of prophetic pictures of the kingdom that is coming on this earth. Psalm 45 presented the coming of the King to establish His kingdom here upon this earth, the millennial kingdom. The following three psalms set before us this kingdom.

This psalm is "To the chief Musician for the sons of Korah, A Song upon Alamoth." The word *almah* is used in Isaiah 7:14 which says, "Therefore the Lord himself shall give you a sign; Behold, a virgin shall conceive, and bear a son, and shall call his name Immanuel." Evidently the word *alamoth* means "with virgins" and in this instance speaks of maidens' voices. This psalm is one of deliverance and will refer us to another great song of deliverance and victory that was sung when the children of Israel crossed the Red Sea. We are told that they sang the song of Moses, but who led the singing? I don't think Moses was a better song leader than I am, and I am no good at all; so Miriam, the prophetess, the sister of Moses and Aaron, took a timbrel in her hand and led the singing. The women went out after her with timbrels and with dances. As Moses and the children of Israel sang, ". . . Miriam answered them, Sing ye to the LORD, for he hath triumphed gloriously; the horse and his rider hath he thrown into the sea" (Exod. 15:21). So the song leader and the soloist on that occasion was Miriam, the sister of Moses. It was the celebration of a great victory.

Now when the future remnant of Israel is delivered from their enemies by the coming of Christ, they will celebrate a great victory. It is important to see this psalm in its proper setting. It belongs after Psalm 45 and with Psalms 47 and 48. To consider these psalms apart from each other is like the little boy who was asked to give a definition of a lie. In his explanation the little fellow put together two Scripture verses that were totally unrelated. He said, "A lie is an abomination unto the Lord, but a very present help in time of trouble." He misinterpreted the Scripture. We smile at the little boy, but we do the same thing by taking this psalm out of context.

Psalm 46 is a wonderful soprano solo. It is not the blues but a hallelujah chorus in which we see the sufficiency of God, the security of God, and the supremacy of God.

THE SUFFICIENCY OF GOD

God is our refuge and strength, a very present help in trouble.

Therefore will not we fear, though the earth be removed, and though the mountains be carried into the midst of the sea;

Though the waters thereof roar and be troubled, though the mountains shake with the swelling thereof. Selah [Ps. 46:1–3].

This is a very wonderful promise. Someone may challenge it and ask, "But how do you know it is true?" Well, it is true because the Bible says so. But it is more than theory with me. I have tried it and found it to be true. We are told, "O taste and see that the LORD is good: blessed is the man that trusteth in him" (Ps. 34:8). Jesus said, "If any man will do his will, he shall know of the doctrine, whether it be of God, or whether I speak of myself" (John 7:17). In times of trouble you can count on God. Christians fail to trust God in times of trouble because they know nothing about His sufficiency. They have not learned that He is sufficient. We need a God who does not fail us. God is sufficient in any circumstance.

"Though the earth be removed"—the removal of the earth would be the most extreme circumstance I can think of. Has the earth ever been taken out from under you? Have you ever been suspended in space? Most people think they are the only ones who have ever had trouble. Everyone has trouble, but God's people find God sufficient in time of trouble. Psalm 46 was Martin Luther's favorite psalm. When he wrote that great Reformation hymn, "A Mighty Fortress Is Our God," he probably had this in mind. God is our refuge, and our strength, and a very present help when we are in trouble. Men down through the ages have found this to be true.

THE SECURITY OF GOD

There is a river, the streams whereof shall make glad the city of God, the holy place of the tabernacles of the most High [Ps. 46:4].

Some expositors consider this river symbolic. I believe the river is a reality that speaks of the supply and the refreshment that God gives even today, and that river is the Word of God. In Psalm 1 we were told that the blessed man was planted by the rivers of water, which is the Word of God. Also the Scriptures mention a river that flows out from the house of God (Ezek. 47). And in the Book of the Revelation John saw ". . . a pure river of water of life, clear as crystal, proceeding out of the throne of God . . ." (Rev. 22:1).

God is in the midst of her; she shall not be moved: God shall help her, and that right early.

The heathen raged, the kingdoms were moved: he uttered his voice, the earth melted.

The LORD of hosts is with us; the God of Jacob is our refuge. Selah [Ps. 46:5–7].

"The heathen raged, the kingdoms were moved" is looking back on the convulsions of the Great Tribulation period. At the darkest hour, when the enemy came in like a flood, "he uttered his voice, the earth melted." Now the faithful remnant who were delivered sing His praises, "The LORD of hosts is with us; the God of Jacob is our refuge."

THE SUPREMACY OF GOD

Come, behold the works of the Lord, what desolations he hath made in the earth.

He maketh wars to cease unto the end of the earth; he breaketh the bow, and cutteth the spear in sunder; he burneth the chariot in the fire [Ps. 46:8–9].

The Messiah has come to the earth in judgment. He is the One who makes wars to cease, breaks the bow, cuts the spear, and burns the chariot in the fire. This picture sets before us the last days on earth, when the One who is ". . . the stone cut out of the mountain without hands . . ." (whom Nebuchadnezzar saw in his vision in Dan. 2:45) will deal an annihilating blow upon this earth. We are told that after the Battle of Armageddon is over, the wreckage of warfare and the dead will be strewn everywhere. The works of God ought to tell man that there is a God. The prediction of peace on earth is here a blessed reality. The King has come and has put down all unrighteousness on the earth.

Be still, and know that I am God: I will be exalted among the heathen, I will be exalted in the earth.

The Lord of hosts is with us; the God of Jacob is our refuge. Selah [Ps. 46:10–11].

"I will be exalted among the heathen [nations], I will be exalted in the earth"—this is God's purpose for the earth.

"Be still, and know that I am God." With the knowledge of this blessed truth we can be calm in time of trouble. There are storms blowing outside today. We are living in a mean old world, a wicked world. Tremendous changes are taking place. There are even convulsions in nature today. He tells us to be calm in the time of storm. Christ, you remember, was in a storm with His disciples, and He went to sleep. When they roused Him from His sleep, He had more trouble calming the disciples than He had calming the storm. Many of us are like those men. We don't know what it is to wait patiently before Him.

This is a psalm that will be a great blessing in the future, but it also is a comfort and a blessing for all of God's people today.

PSALM 47

THEME: Praise and worship in the Millennium

This is the second of the little cluster of prophetic pictures of the millennial kingdom, which is established by the Lord Jesus Christ at His second coming. This is a continuation of praise and worship of Christ who is now King over all the earth.

> **O clap your hands, all ye people; shout unto God with the voice of triumph.**
>
> **For the LORD most high is terrible; he is a great King over all the earth [Ps. 47:1–2].**

"The LORD most high is terrible [awe-inspiring]; he is a great King over all the earth"—you see, Christ is reigning as King over all the earth; and as such, He is praised and worshipped.

My friend, before Christ can reign on this earth, He will have to put down all rebellion, self-conceit, arrogance, and the lawlessness of man against God. In Psalm 46 we saw the celebration of His coming in judgment, and now in Psalm 47 His kingdom is established and He is reigning on the earth.

> **He shall subdue the people under us, and the nations under our feet.**
>
> **He shall choose our inheritance for us, the excellency of Jacob whom he loved. Selah [Ps. 47:3–4].**

This is the appropriate time to sing, "Joy to the World!"

> Joy to the world! the Lord is come;
> Let earth receive her King;

Let every heart prepare Him room,
And heav'n and nature sing.

Joy to the world! the Saviour reigns;
Let men their songs employ;
While fields and floods, rocks, hills and
   plains
Repeat the sounding joy.

No more let sins and sorrows grow,
Nor thorns infest the ground;
He comes to make His blessings flow
Far as the curse is found.

He rules the world with truth and grace,
And makes the nations prove
The glories of His righteousness,
And wonders of His love.
                              —Isaac Watts

As you can see, this is not really a hymn that speaks of the birth of
Christ; but it speaks of His second coming. There is going to be joy on
the earth when He comes.

"Clap your hands; . . . shout unto God with the voice of triumph!"
What a wonderful day that will be!

Not long ago I preached in a church where the people clapped
their hands and were rather vociferous. Later someone asked me if all
the noise did not disturb me. I replied, "No, it helped a great deal
because they were right with me." I think that what many people call
reverence today is really deadness. There is a lot of reverence in the
cemetery—no one disturbs anybody or anything. I believe we need a
little life in our services.

**God is gone up with a shout, the LORD with the sound of
a trumpet.**

**Sing praises to God, sing praises: sing praises unto our
King, sing praises.**

For God is the King of all the earth: sing ye praises with understanding.

God reigneth over the heathen: God sitteth upon the throne of his holiness.

The princes of the people are gathered together, even the people of the God of Abraham: for the shields of the earth belong unto God: he is greatly exalted [Ps. 47:5-9].

Let me give you Dr. Gaebelein's translation of this passage. "God is gone up amidst shouting, Jehovah amid the sound of a trumpet. Sing Psalms unto God! Sing Psalms unto our King, sing Psalms! For God is the King of all the earth—sing Psalms for instruction. God reigneth over the nations; God sitteth upon the throne of His holiness. The willing hearted of the people have gathered together with the people of the God of Abraham; for unto God belong the shields of the earth; He is greatly exalted" (The Book of Psalms, p. 207).

"God is gone up with a shout, the LORD with the sound of a trumpet"—that is, He has ascended amid shouting. And the fact that He ascended means He made a previous descent. The Lord came to earth nineteen hundred years ago, was born in Bethlehem, finished His work of salvation on earth, and then ascended to heaven—I think Psalm 24 refers to that. But in this psalm another ascension is spoken about. When Christ comes to earth the second time, He will establish His kingdom and be going back and forth to the New Jerusalem. I think that between the New Jerusalem and this earth there is going to be a freeway much busier than any of the California freeways—with one exception: there will be no traffic tie-ups. You will be able to move back and forth with freedom. Probably the Lord will descend and ascend at stated times during the Millennium and will display His visible glory upon the earth.

What a glorious, wonderful prospect this psalm predicts!

PSALM 48

THEME: Messiah's final victory upon the earth

This is the last of the group of three millennial psalms. It celebrates the final and complete victory of the Messiah.

> Great is the LORD, and greatly to be praised in the city of our God, in the mountain of his holiness.
>
> Beautiful for situation, the joy of the whole earth, is mount Zion, on the sides of the north, the city of the great King.
>
> God is known in her palaces for a refuge [Ps. 48:1–3].

Once again, I would like to give Dr. Gaebelein's translation. "Great is Jehovah, and greatly to be praised, in the city of our God, in His holy mountain. Beautiful in elevation, the joy of the whole earth, is the Mount Zion, the sides of the north, the city of the great King. God in her palaces hath made Himself known as a high tower" (*The Book of Psalms,* p. 208).

When it says Mount Zion, it means Mount Zion; and when it talks about the city of God in the holy mountain, it refers to Jerusalem.

Note the mention of "the sides of the north." This is an interesting expression. It probably speaks of a way of ascent and descent to this earth. There is a remarkable prophecy in Isaiah which mentions Satan in connection with "the sides of the north": "For thou hast said in thine heart, I will ascend into heaven, I will exalt my throne above the stars of God: I will sit also upon the mount of the congregation, in the sides of the north: I will ascend above the heights of the clouds; I will be like the most High" (Isa. 14:13–14). The "sides of the north" is apparently the route. Satan actually hoped to overthrow God!

This now is the conflict which is the last great battle that will take place on the earth:

> For, lo, the kings were assembled, they passed by to-
> gether.
>
> They saw it, and so they marvelled; they were troubled,
> and hasted away [Ps. 48:4–5].

Notice Dr. Gaebelein's translation through verse 7: "For lo! the kings
were gathered, they passed by together. They saw it and were amazed;
they were terror stricken, they started to flee, trembling came upon
them there, pains as a woman in travail. With the East wind Thou hast
broken the ships of Tarshish" (*The Book of Psalms*, p. 209). I believe it
describes the time after the thousand years of peace when the devil is
released for a season: "And when the thousand years are expired, Satan shall be loosed out of his prison, And shall go out to deceive the
nations which are in the four quarters of the earth, Gog and Magog, to
gather them together to battle: the number of whom is as the sand of
the sea. And they went up on the breadth of the earth, and compassed
the camp of the saints about, and the beloved city: and fire came down
from God out of heaven, and devoured them" (Rev. 20:7–9).

> As we have heard, so have we seen in the city of the LORD
> of hosts, in the city of our God: God will establish it for
> ever. Selah [Ps. 48:8].

The people have heard and read all about this from their prophets,
and now they are seeing the literal accomplishment of it all. It is the
promised deliverance that down through the centuries God has as-
sured them was coming. Finally it is realized.

> We have thought of thy lovingkindness, O God, in the
> midst of thy temple.
>
> According to thy name, O God, so is thy praise unto the
> ends of the earth: thy right hand is full of righteousness
> [Ps. 48:9–10].

In their millennial temple they will worship Him and meditate upon
His lovingkindness to them.

This psalm concludes with a great hallelujah chorus.

> **Let mount Zion rejoice, let the daughters of Judah be
> glad, because of thy judgments.**
>
> **Walk about Zion, and go round about her: tell the towers
> thereof.**
>
> **Mark ye well her bulwarks, consider her palaces; that
> ye may tell it to the generation following.**
>
> **For this God is our God for ever and ever: he will be our
> guide even unto death [Ps. 48:11-14].**

With great joy they will walk about Jerusalem, noticing every part of
it, and praise Him who is their God and guide of their lives. What
praise this will be!

PSALM 49

THEME: *The end of those who boast themselves in riches*

Psalm 49 concludes this first segment of the Exodus section of Psalms. We have seen the vindication of God's ways in connection with the wicked and the righteous. We have seen that God leads His people who are away from Him and out of the land. He has made known His intention of bringing His own to Himself and keeping them during the time of great trouble, just as He brought His people out of the land of Egypt when they were in bondage under a dictator.

Psalm 49 is designed to contrast the ways of God in dealing with the wicked and the righteous. It does not exactly philosophize about the uncertainty of riches, the shortness of life; it is not just a sweet little dissertation which bids us bear bravely our perils and our sufferings, and tells us that virtue is its own reward, and that justice will triumph at the end. Rather, this psalm shows us not only the vanity of riches but the end of those who boast themselves in riches. This psalm may sound a bit revolutionary to you according to the thinking of today, but it is one that should be given special consideration in the days in which we live.

> Hear this, all ye people; give ear, all ye inhabitants of the world:
>
> Both low and high, rich and poor, together.
>
> My mouth shall speak of wisdom; and the meditation of my heart shall be of understanding.
>
> I will incline mine ear to a parable: I will open my dark saying upon the harp [Ps. 49:1–4].

Or, as Dr. Gaebelein has translated them: "Hear ye this, all ye peoples, give ear, all ye inhabitants of the age, both low and high, rich and poor together! My mouth speaketh wisdom, and the meditation of my heart is understanding. I will incline mine ear to a parable. I will open my riddle upon the harp" (*The Book of Psalms*, p. 211).

What the psalmist is doing in this psalm, and will also do in the next one, is issuing a call to God's creatures to "hear." We are going to see this same thing when we come to the first chapter of Isaiah. We have already seen this in the Book of Deuteronomy. You will recall that when the Lord was ready to put His people in the land which He had promised, He called heaven and earth to witness that He was not only giving His people the land, but the conditions under which He was giving it to them. He used the form of a song. "Give ear, O ye heavens, and I will speak; and hear, O earth, the words of my mouth" (Deut. 32:1). This is the beginning of the song of Moses. In this song, God calls heaven and earth to witness the conditions under which He is putting them in the land. At least eight hundred years later, God is ready to put His people out of the land because of their sin. Again, in the Book of Isaiah, God calls heaven and earth to witness that putting His people out of the land is just and righteous (Isa. 1:2).

Now here is God's call to hear something that may be troubling you also, and it begins with a question:

Wherefore should I fear in the days of evil, when the iniquity of my heels shall compass me about? [Ps. 49:5].

Immediately you wonder who is asking the question. Is it the psalmist? Or is this question asked by the self-confident rich? Perhaps it is asked by the righteous who suffer unjustly at the hands of the wicked, or asked by the people today who are in want. I believe it is the question of a poor man. I was a poor boy, and I confess that I have always considered the rich with a little bit of suspicion. I question their motives. Why does God permit some people to become so rich? What is going to happen to them? Why do they get by with so much and seem not to have the same troubles as other men? There is a clique today in this country that is made up of the rich and influential. At election time they talk to us and tell us how wonderful, intelligent, and lovely we are because they want us to vote for their candidates. The question is, Why does God permit them to get by with so much? Why doesn't God do something about it?" Let's see what this psalm has to say about this subject.

> **They that trust in their wealth, and boast themselves in the multitude of their riches;**
>
> **None of them can by any means redeem his brother, nor give to God a ransom for him [Ps. 49:6-7].**

No matter how rich a man is, he cannot buy salvation. He and I go to the counter for salvation. I have nothing with which to buy salvation. The rich man has money, but he cannot buy salvation with it. We are both on the same par. The rich man is excluded from redemption if he is deluded into thinking that he can either buy, do something, or give something to obtain his salvation. Romans 4:5 says, "But to him that worketh not, but believeth on him that justifieth the ungodly, his faith is counted for righteousness."

Now we come to a parenthesis.

> **(For the redemption of their soul is precious, and it ceaseth for ever:) [Ps. 49:8].**

They don't have enough money to buy their salvation—no one has enough to buy his salvation.

> **That he should still live for ever, and not see corruption [Ps. 49:9].**

Those who are rich will die just like everyone else. I think it was on the basis of this psalm that the Lord Jesus gave the parable about the rich man and Lazarus, the poor man, as recorded in Luke 16:19-26. No man, regardless of how rich he is, can redeem his (or another's) soul so that he can have eternal life.

> **For he seeth that wise men die, likewise the fool and the brutish person perish, and leave their wealth to others [Ps. 49:10].**

I don't care who you are, or how much wealth you have accumulated, some day you will die and leave it all behind. You can take all your treasures and put them in a safety deposit box, or in a vault, or bury them in the earth; you can say, "This is mine. Nobody can take it away from me." You are right—no one can take it away from you, but there is Someone who can take you away from it. He is the Lord. One day death will knock at your door, and at that time you will be as poor as anyone. As the old bromide puts it, there is no pocket in a shroud.

Years ago when one of the Astors died, some of the eager relatives were waiting outside. When the lawyer came out, they asked, "How much did he leave?" The lawyer replied, "He left it all." He did not take anything with him. That is the first thing the psalmist observes— the rich "leave their wealth to others." Friend, you may be rich while you are here on earth, but you cannot buy salvation, nor can you extend your life on earth forever. Someday you will have to leave, and that bundle you made here will have to stay. That is one reason we encourage people to leave what they have accumulated to Christian work to get the Word of God out to needy hearts. That is what is important.

> **Their inward thought is, that their houses shall continue for ever, and their dwelling places to all generations; they call their lands after their own names [Ps. 49:11].**

Many people try to perpetuate their names. I think it is interesting that the Rockefeller name is on buildings all over the world. People say, "My, wasn't he generous." In one sense that is pretty cheap advertising. I have never been able to pay enough money to have my name put in marble on a building—I don't want it there either. The point is that a name on a building doesn't mean much. One of these days the buildings are going to come down, and the individual will be forgotten.

> **Nevertheless man being in honour abideth not: he is like the beasts that perish [Ps. 49:12].**

Men who have held high positions will go into the grave and return to dust just like everyone else.

This their way is their folly: yet their posterity approve their sayings. Selah [Ps. 49:13].

Now here is a very interesting expression:

Like sheep they are laid in the grave; death shall feed on them; and the upright shall have dominion over them in the morning; and their beauty shall consume in the grave from their dwelling [Ps. 49:14].

The word *grave* in verse 14 is "Sheol, or the world of the dead." The rich, like sheep, are laid in Sheol. The literal rendering is: *death* is their shepherd. In contrast to this David said, "The LORD is my shepherd" (Ps. 23:1) and He is *life.* "He that hath the Son hath life; and he that hath not the Son of God hath not life" (1 John 5:12). The false shepherd is death. "Death shall feed on them." That is interesting. A shepherd should feed his sheep, but here is a shepherd who is eating his sheep.

We are also told that "their beauty shall consume in the grave [Sheol] from their dwelling." A person may spend a fortune in a beauty parlor. A person may put on all kinds of lotions, powders, and creams; but what they look like after a few years in the grave is not a pretty sight. I have seen several like that. Death is not a beautiful thing by any means.

But God will redeem my soul from the power of the grave [Sheol]: for he shall receive me. Selah [Ps. 49:15].

"Selah" indicates a pause at this point so that you can think over what you have read. God alone is able to redeem your soul. The important thing in this life is not whether you are rich or poor. In the final analysis, when you move out into eternity, the important thing is whether or not you are redeemed, whether or not you are a child of God through faith in Christ:

> **Be not thou afraid when one is made rich, when the glory of his house is increased [Ps. 49:16].**

Rich people today are getting away with murder, and with adultery, and with all kinds of things, and they are elected to office. Poor people are not getting a just deal in this world today. One of the reasons I cast my lot with the Lord Jesus is because He is going to judge the poor in righteousness. Some day I know I am going to get a fair deal.

> **For when he dieth he shall carry nothing away: his glory shall not descend after him.**

> **Though while he lived he blessed his soul: and men will praise thee, when thou doest well to thyself.**

> **He shall go to the generation of his fathers; they shall never see light.**

> **Man that is in honour, and understandeth not, is like the beasts that perish [Ps. 49:17–20].**

This is an interesting passage. We hear a great deal today about the theory that man has evolved from beasts and animals. The fact of the matter is that the Bible teaches the opposite. God created man in an upright position. God created man in His image. Man fell, and man can so live apart from God that he is like an animal in his life, and he is like an animal when he dies. Man does not evolve upward; he devolves downward. He is not on the upward trail at all. His inclination is to go down. That is natural with anything in this life. Everything, in my judgment, contradicts evolution. Nothing goes upward by itself; it all gravitates downward. The law of gravitation in the physical world pulls everything down. There is also a moral law of gravitation, which is immorality, and it will pull a man down.

My friend, let's not be disturbed when we see the wicked prospering.

PSALM 50

THEME: A psalm of judgment

This is the first psalm of Asaph, a musician and one of the three song leaders in the temple. Heman, Asaph, and Ethan were the three.

This is a great psalm of judgment. It reveals God coming in righteousness to judge His people and to judge the wicked.

> **The mighty God, even the LORD, hath spoken, and called the earth from the rising of the sun unto the going down thereof.**
>
> **Out of Zion, the perfection of beauty, God hath shined.**
>
> **Our God shall come, and shall not keep silence: a fire shall devour before him, and it shall be very tempestuous round about him [Ps. 50:1–3].**

The introduction to this psalm proclaims that the mighty God is coming. What a glorious anticipation this should be for the child of God. Some day we shall *see* our Lord! That is the prospect for every believer.

> **He shall call to the heavens from above, and to the earth, that he may judge his people [Ps. 50:4].**

When God is getting ready to judge, He wants plenty of witnesses to be there to make sure that He is righteous in all that He does. He says:

> **Gather my saints together unto me; those that have made a covenant with me by sacrifice [Ps. 50:5].**

Those saints who have made a covenant with God by sacrifice are the Jews, the children of Israel.

**And the heavens shall declare his righteousness: for
God is judge himself. Selah [Ps. 50:6].**

The Lord Jesus Christ is going to be the judge. "For the Father judgeth
no man, but hath committed all judgment unto the Son" (John 5:22).

**Hear, O my people, and I will speak; O Israel, and I will
testify against thee: I am God, even thy God [Ps. 50:7].**

If you had lived in Jerusalem when the temple was there and people
worshiped in it, you probably would have asked, "Lord, are you criticizing these people? They come regularly to the temple (which is the
equivalent of every Sunday morning and evening service plus prayer
meeting on Wednesday night). They are as busy as termites serving
around the temple." Sure they were, but just going to church is not the
most important thing. Of course it is important, but it will not establish a relationship with God. You had better establish that relationship through Christ so that your churchgoing can be pleasing to God.

**I will not reprove thee for thy sacrifices or thy burnt of-
ferings, to have been continually before me.**

**I will take no bullock out of thy house, nor he goats out
of thy folds.**

**For every beast of the forest is mine, and the cattle upon
a thousand hills [Ps. 50:8–10].**

God says, "Did you really think you were giving Me something when
you brought sacrifices to Me? Why, all the animals belong to Me any-
way." This reminds us of the words of Jeremiah the prophet: "For I
spake not unto your fathers, nor commanded them in the day that I
brought them out of the land of Egypt, concerning burnt offerings or
sacrifices: But this thing commanded I them, saying, Obey my voice,
and I will be your God, and ye shall be my people: and walk ye in all
the ways that I have commanded you, that it may be well unto you"
(Jer. 7:22–23). The prophet Micah said something similar: "Where-

with shall I come before the Lord, and bow myself before the high
God? shall I come before him with burnt offerings, with calves of a
year old? Will the Lord be pleased with thousands of rams, or with ten
thousands of rivers of oil? shall I give my firstborn for my transgression, the fruit of my body for the sin of my soul? He hath shewed thee,
O man, what is good; and what doth the Lord require of thee, but to do
justly, and to love mercy, and to walk humbly with thy God?" (Mic.
6:6–8).

> **If I were hungry, I would not tell thee: for the world is
> mine, and the fulness thereof [Ps. 50:12].**

If the Creator were hungry, He certainly would not need to tell the
creature about it!

> **And call upon me in the day of trouble: I will deliver
> thee, and thou shalt glorify me [Ps. 50:15].**

God asks His people to come to Him. But God intends to judge the
wicked. He is saying, "I didn't intend to let you get by with sin."

> **These things hast thou done, and I kept silence; thou
> thoughtest that I was altogether such an one as thyself:
> but I will reprove thee, and set them in order before
> thine eyes.**

> **Now consider this, ye that forget God, lest I tear you in
> pieces, and there be none to deliver [Ps. 50:21–22].**

My friend, God is not speaking only to Israel, He is speaking to us in
our day also. He unmasks hypocrisy. Because God is silent does not
mean that He approves. There is a day of reckoning coming. God says,
"I will reprove thee, and set them [your sins] in order before thine
eyes."

But God never ceases to be gracious. The way of salvation is mentioned.

**Whoso offereth praise glorifieth me: and to him that or-
dereth his conversation aright will I shew the salvation
of God [Ps. 50:23].**

"To him that ordereth his conversation [his way] aright"—who con-
fesses his sins to God—will be shown the way of salvation.

PSALM 51

THEME: David's great penitential psalm

The superscription on many of the psalms is actually a part of the inspired Word of God. The title of Psalm 51 is self-explanatory, and it is essential to the understanding of this psalm. "To the chief Musician, A Psalm of David, when Nathan the prophet came unto him, after he had gone in to Bathsheba." The reference, of course, is to the great blot on David's life. It is not our intention to go into the lurid details of David's sin. Suffice it to say that David broke two of God's commandments. He broke the seventh commandment: "Thou shalt not commit adultery." He did with Bathsheba. He broke the sixth commandment: "Thou shalt not kill." He broke it indirectly in that he arranged for Uriah, the husband of Bathsheba, to be put in the front of the battle that he might be killed. And this was a dastardly and cold-blooded deal on the part of David, because Uriah was one of his mighty men and one of his most faithful followers—or he would never have gone into the front of the battle at David's command.

Now after this disgraceful incident, David did nothing, and he said nothing. Actually, both incidents would be considered business as usual down in Egypt, or in Babylon, or in Philistia, or in Edom, or in Moab. What David had done was a common practice and was more or less accepted. As a great preacher of the South said years ago, "When you put together a bunch of crooked sticks, they seem to straighten each other out." Have you ever noted that? And in this case when many monarchs engaged in things like this it gave it an air of not being as bad as it was. But it was as bad as God said it was.

On the surface it looked as if David had gotten by with it. But let's put down one thing: David was God's man, and David was not going to get by with it. The fact of the matter is, during the interval when he kept quiet, he was a tormented man. He told us later what really went on in his heart. Over in Psalm 32, David says this: "When I kept silence, my bones waxed old through my roaring all the day long" (Ps. 32:3). I think if you'd been in the court of David during that period when he was silent, you would have seen him age. This man went through awful anxiety. "For day and night thy hand was heavy upon me: my moisture is turned into the drought of summer" (Ps. 32:4). This describes his feelings during that interval.

Then God sent Nathan to David demanding an audience regarding an urgent matter. And Nathan approached the subject by telling David a story: "And the LORD sent Nathan unto David. And he came unto him, and said unto him, There were two men in one city; the one rich, and the other poor. The rich man had exceeding many flocks and herds: But the poor man had nothing, save one little ewe lamb, which he had bought and nourished up: and it grew up together with him, and with his children; it did eat of his own meat, and drank of his own cup, and lay in his bosom, and was unto him as a daughter. And there came a traveller unto the rich man, and he spared to take of his own flock and of his own herd, to dress for the wayfaring man that was come unto him; but took the poor man's lamb, and dressed it for the man that was come to him. And David's anger was greatly kindled against the man; and he said to Nathan, As the LORD liveth, the man that hath·done this thing shall surely die: And he shall restore the lamb fourfold, because he did this thing, and because he had no pity" (2 Sam. 12:1-6).

Then we come to one of the most dramatic moments in the Word of God, and it reveals Nathan as one of the bravest men in Scripture: "And Nathan said to David, Thou art the man . . ." (2 Sam. 12:7). Nathan pointed his finger at David and said to him, "You're the man!"

When he said that, there were three courses open to David. He could deny the charge. He could say, "Nathan is entirely wrong and is attempting to smear me." Or he could have merely pointed his scepter at Nathan, without saying a word because the guards would have understood, and would have led Nathan out and summarily executed him. David would not have needed to say anything. And, I suppose, if it had been carried to any kind of tribunal (which in those days it would not have been), the "supreme court" would have handed down a decision that undue pressure was used by Nathan to extract a confession from David, and David would have been freed from all charges.

There was a third course open to David, and that was to admit the charge. David followed the latter course. He made confession of his sin. Now David was not just a man; he was the king. And the king can do no wrong; he is above reproach. No one points the finger at the king. But Nathan did. And the very interesting thing is that David confessed.

Now continuing with this encounter, let's pick up at verse 10, with Nathan giving him God's message: "Now therefore the sword shall never depart from thine house; because thou hast despised me, and hast taken the wife of Uriah the Hittite to be thy wife. Thus saith the LORD, Behold, I will raise up evil against thee out of thine own house, and I will take thy wives before thine eyes, and give them unto thy neighbor, and he shall lie with thy wives in the sight of this sun. For thou didst it secretly: but I will do this thing before all Israel, and before the sun. And David said unto Nathan, I have sinned against the LORD. And Nathan said unto David, The LORD also hath put away thy sin; thou shalt not die. Howbeit, because of this deed thou hast given great occasion to the enemies of the LORD to blaspheme, the child also that is born unto thee shall surely die" (2 Sam. 12:10–14).

This now is the background of Psalm 51, because after this, David went into the privacy of his own chamber and made the confession which this psalm records.

All the great men of God have confessed their sin before God. Augustine wrote his confessions. But Psalm 51 is one of the greatest confessionals that has ever been written.

Psalm 51 divides very nicely into three divisions: (1) Cry of Conscience and Conviction of Sin—verses 1–3; (2) Cry of Confession of Sin and Clemency (Compassion) of God—verses 4–8; (3) Cry for Cleansing and Communion—verses 9–19.

CRY OF CONSCIENCE AND CONVICTION OF SIN

Let us now listen to David's confession:

Have mercy upon me, O God, according to thy lovingkindness: according unto the multitude of thy tender
mercies blot out my transgressions.

Wash me thoroughly from mine iniquity, and cleanse
me from my sin.

For I acknowledge my transgressions: and my sin is
ever before me [Ps. 51:1–3].

Sin is always complicated. It never is simple. And there are several
words that David uses to describe his sin. In the Scriptures God uses
many more words than this to describe sin, by the way. Sin is that
which is complicated; it is goodness that is simple. Let me give you
an illustration. Suppose I were holding behind me a stick and I told
you it was a crooked stick. How do you think it would look? No two
people would think it looked like it really does. No two would agree
because it could be crooked in a million different ways. But suppose I
say that I hold a ruler behind me that is perfectly straight. Everyone
would think of it in just one way. It can't be straight in more than one
way. It is sin that is complicated; it is goodness that is simple.

David, first of all, called his sins *transgressions*. To transgress is to
step over the boundaries of God. God has put up certain boundaries in
this life. He has certain physical laws. He has certain moral laws. He
has certain spiritual laws. Any time man attempts to step over any of
them, he'll have to suffer the consequences. To do this is always
called transgression.

Also David called his sin *iniquity*. And *iniquity* means that which
is altogether wrong. You can't excuse it; you can't offer some sort of an
apology for it; you can't in any way condone it. That's *iniquity*. Then
there are two words translated with the English word *sin*. In verses 2
and 3 it is the Hebrew word *chattath*, meaning "sin offering." In
verse 4 it is *chata*, translated in the Septuagint by the Greek word
hamartia, meaning "to miss the mark." That's all—just miss the
mark. We don't come up to God's standard, and it is in that sense that
all of us today are sinners. None of us come up to the standard of God.
"For all have sinned, and come short of the glory of God" (Rom. 3:23).

Then the word *evil* that is used here by David means that which is actually wrong. In our day we even have ministers who are trying to condone all kinds of immorality, but let it be understood that the Bible is still very clear on what is right and what is wrong. There are questionable areas on which the Bible is silent, I grant you, but there is also clear-cut black and clear-cut white. God is unmistakably certain on these things. *Evil* is that which is actually wrong. David uses this word to speak of the fact that he was wrong. He admitted it.

There is a dispensational aspect to this psalm, but I am not going to deal with that here. Actually, you cannot cram this psalm into one dispensation. It voices the experience of a man who is a member of the human family. This is the experience of a man in *any* dispensation— at any time since Adam and Eve left the Garden of Eden and on until eternity begins on this earth.

The experience of David is that he has come under deep conviction of sin. You and I cannot enter into the horror of the guilt of David. To him his sin was repugnant. He hated it, and he hated himself because he did it. He felt dirty all over. His conscience was outraged. And he had a feeling of guilt as big as the Rock of Gibraltar. There was anguish of soul in this man. Conscience was pointing an accusing finger at him, and there was a cry of conscience within, telling David he was wrong.

Now I know someone will say, "But conscience is not a good guide." That's true. But let's notice that conscience has a function; the function of conscience is not to tell us what is right or what is wrong. That is not the purpose of conscience. The purpose of conscience, and the function of it, is to tell us that we *are* right or that we *are* wrong. It doesn't tell us what is right and wrong. Let me give you an example in the New Testament. Paul uses it in his letter to the Corinthians: "Whatsoever is sold in the shambles, that eat, asking no question for conscience sake: For the earth is the Lord's, and the fulness thereof" (1 Cor. 10:25–26). Then he goes on to say: "Conscience, I say, not thine own, but of the other . . ." (1 Cor. 10:29). What Paul is saying is this: "As far as God is concerned whether you eat meat or you don't eat meat makes no difference. But if you go into the home of someone and meat is served to you, don't ask them where they bought it. If you

knew they bought it at the heathen temple, then your conscience
would tell you that you were wrong in eating it—because you may
have a wrong influence. But if you don't know, if your host doesn't
tell you, then it's not wrong for you to eat it." Conscience, you see,
doesn't tell you *what* is wrong; it tells you that it *is* wrong. There are
some folk who have a conscience about one thing and some have a
conscience about something else. And it is dangerous for any person
to violate his own conscience.

Now David's conscience was speaking to him, and the cry of his
conscience was a conviction of sin. He was wrong, and there was no
explanation he could offer at all. Listen to him:

> **For I acknowledge my transgressions: and my sin is
> ever before me [Ps. 51:3].**

The king said he was wrong.

CRY OF CONFESSION OF SIN AND CLEMENCY (COMPASSION) OF GOD

The second division is the cry of confession of sin, and the clemency
and compassion of God.

> **Against thee, thee only, have I sinned, and done this evil
> in thy sight: that thou mightest be justified when thou
> speakest, and be clear when thou judgest [Ps. 51:4].**

David has been criticized because he made this statement. There are
those who say he should not have said it was a sin against God; he
should have said it was a sin against Bathsheba. Wasn't it? It sure was.
Also it was a sin against his family, for he had a family at that time. It
was a sin against them, and David should have said that, so the critics
say. They also say that it was a sin against society and Jerusalem at that
time, and it was. It was a sin against the nation of which he was king.
He was breaking God's commandment. But, my friend, in the final

analysis sin is always against God. Bathsheba is gone. I do not know where her family is. The society of that day has disappeared. Actually, the nation is no longer under the line of David. But that sin still stands on the escutcheon of the Word of God and against God.

Let's read the historical record again, as it is very important. This is what God said to David: "Now therefore the sword shall never depart from thine house; because thou hast despised me, and hast taken the wife of Uriah the Hittite to be thy wife" (2 Sam. 12:10). "And David said unto Nathan, I have sinned against the LORD. And Nathan said unto David, The LORD also hath put away thy sin; thou shalt not die. Howbeit, because by this deed thou hast given great occasion to the enemies of the LORD to blaspheme, the child also that is born unto thee shall surely die" (2 Sam. 12:13–14). For three thousand years now the enemy, the critic, has been pointing his finger at the Word of God and saying, "You mean to tell me that David is a man after God's own heart?" I heard this on Pershing Square in Los Angeles several years ago. A man had gathered around him a crowd—he was a disheveled, dirty-looking fellow, with a leer in his voice and on his face. He said to them, "Now they say God is holy!" Then he gave a suggestive laugh and made some filthy statements about David, and said, "They say He is a holy God!"

God said to David, "David, you've hurt Me." One night I went with some friends to Bughouse Square in Chicago (that corresponds to Pershing Square in Los Angeles, and that's a better name than Pershing Square, by the way), and there was the worst filth I've ever heard. I never have heard a man as filthy as he was. And who was he talking about? David. God said, "David, you've given great occasion to My enemies to blaspheme, and because of that the child will die, and the sword will never leave your house." And it never did. To his dying day David paid for his sin. Not only *that* child died, but the son he loved, the one he wanted to succeed him as king, also died. When David heard that his son Absalom had been killed in battle, he wrapped his mantle about his head, walked to the top of the wall, up those winding stairs, and as he went up he wept, ". . . O my son Absalom, my son, my son Absalom! would God I had died for thee, O Absalom, my son, my son!" (2 Sam. 18:33). David did not think Absalom was saved; he wanted him to live. My friend, David paid for his sin.

Now notice that David makes it very clear that this sin goes back to a sin nature.

Behold, I was shapen in iniquity; and in sin did my mother conceive me [Ps. 51:5].

David, as well as the rest of us, came into the world with a sin nature. Paul, recognizing this, says to believers today, "Brethren, if a [Christian] man be overtaken in a fault, ye which are spiritual, restore such an one in the spirit of meekness; considering thyself, lest thou also be tempted" (Gal. 6:1). And Goethe said that he saw no fault committed which he too might not have committed. And Samuel Johnson said, "Every man knows that of himself which he dares not tell his dearest friend." Even Seneca, a pagan philosopher of Rome, said, "We must say of ourselves that we are evil, have been evil, and unhappily, I must add—shall be also in the future. Nobody can deliver himself; someone must stretch out a hand to lift him up." And the Word of God confirms this. Even the writer of Ecclesiastes says, "For there is not a just man upon earth, that doeth good, and sinneth not" (Eccl. 7:20). Also in the Book of Proverbs we read, "There is a generation that are pure in their own eyes, and yet is not washed from their filthiness" (Prov. 30:12). There are people who think they are all right, but they are not sensitive to sin. They are like the man in the far North who, as he got colder, wanted to rest. He felt very comfortable sitting down. But those with him knew what was happening to him—he was freezing to death. They wouldn't let him sit down but kept him moving so he would not die. Today there are many sitting in our churches so cold and so comfortable that they do not realize that in God's sight they are sinners. We not only need a Savior, but we need *cleansing*. Paul says, "For I know that in me (that is, in my flesh,) dwelleth no good thing . . ." (Rom. 7:18). David, you see, went right down to the root of the matter. He confessed that he had a sin nature.

David's confession continues:

**Behold, thou desirest truth in the inward parts: and in
the hidden part thou shalt make me to know wisdom
[Ps. 51:6].**

God is not interested in what you have been on the surface. You may
be baptized and be nothing more than a baptized sinner, still un-
saved. You may be a member of a church, but, my friend, that is all
exterior. You still could be lost. He says He desires truth on the inside.
The psalmist goes on:

**Purge me with hyssop, and I shall be clean: wash me,
and I shall be whiter than snow [Ps. 51:7].**

Follow me now very carefully. Here is without doubt one of the greatest passages in the Word of God. There are those who say that the
reason David was forgiven was because he confessed his sin. If you
say that, you've told only part of the story. That's not the reason. Turn
back to the historical record: "And David said unto Nathan, I have
sinned against the LORD. And Nathan said unto David, The LORD also
hath put away thy sin; thou shalt not die" (2 Sam. 12:13). God took
the first step: He sent Nathan. I think David would still be sitting over
there keeping quiet if Nathan had not come in. Maybe he couldn't
have kept it much longer—I don't know. But he didn't make the first
step; God made the first step.

And how was God able to forgive him? Because He had revealed
Himself. Now follow this closely. God revealed Himself to the nation
Israel: "And the LORD passed by before him, and proclaimed, The
LORD, The LORD God, merciful and gracious, longsuffering, and abun-
dant in goodness and truth, Keeping mercy for thousands, forgiving
iniquity and transgression and sin, and that will by no means clear
the guilty; visiting the iniquity of the fathers upon the children, and
upon the children's children, unto the third and to the fourth generation" (Exod. 34:6–7). Somebody asks, "Doesn't it go any further than
that?" It sure does. It will keep going, but that is as far down as any
man will be able to see—the third and fourth generations. A man may

see his sin carried down that far. But I want you to notice here two things that are conflicting and contradictory. God says He forgives iniquity and He shows mercy. Then He turns right around and says, "that will by no means clear the guilty." There is a paradox. Listen to David again: "Purge me with hyssop, and I shall be clean: wash me, and I shall be whiter than snow." Hyssop was a little plant that grew on rocks in damp places. An interesting sidelight is a statement from a scientific journal that penicillin was found growing on hyssop. However, hyssop had to do with something penicillin can't cure: sin. Back in the Old Testament hyssop was used for three purposes. First, when God took the children of Israel out of Egypt, He said, "There is one thing you must do at the Passover. You are to take a lamb, slay it and take its blood in a basin out to the front door and, with bunches of hyssop, apply the blood to the doorposts and to the lintel, then go back inside." Second, when God was giving instructions for cleansing a leper, He told about taking two birds. One was to be slain; the live bird was taken with hyssop, dipped in the blood of the slain bird, and then let fly away. This portrays the death and resurrection of Christ. But the application of it was by hyssop. Third, when the people of Israel were on the wilderness march and one of them sinned, they couldn't stop and put up the tabernacle and offer a sacrifice. So provisions were made for purification of sin by killing a red heifer, burning it (with hyssop added), gathering the ashes and taking them along on the wilderness march. When a man sinned, the ashes were put in water, then hyssop was used to sprinkle them on him. There was the application of a sacrifice that brought forgiveness.

You have to go to the cross to find the interpretation. On the cross the Son of God said, ". . . My God, my God, why hast thou forsaken me?" (Matt. 27:46). Why did He say that? I'll tell you why. Because God *cannot by any means clear the guilty.* He can't. He never will. And when the Lord Jesus Christ, on the cross, was made sin for us, He who knew no sin, that we might be made the righteousness of God in Him—when He was delivered for our offenses—God had to treat Him as He *must* treat sin. God spared Abraham's son; but God did not spare His own Son when He had my sin and your sin upon Him. He

had to slay Him, because God *cannot* pardon the guilty. Let's be clear
on that. He does not operate like our Supreme Court. God *hates* sin.
God will punish sin. By no means will He clear the guilty. And His
Son *died*.

On the cross Jesus also said, ". . . Father, forgive them . . ." (Luke
23:34). *Forgive* them! How can He forgive them? How can He extend
mercy to thousands? How can He forgive iniquity? How can He forgive David? And how can He forgive you and me? "In whom we have
redemption through his blood, the forgiveness of sins, according to
the riches of his grace" (Eph. 1:7). And every time you find forgiveness in the New Testament, the blood of Christ is close by. God never
forgives sin apart from the death of Christ. Never. *Never.* God is not
forgiving sin because He is big-hearted. He forgives because His Son
paid the penalty. And now with open arms He can say to you, "I can
extend mercy to *you* because my Son died for you." Oh, David knew
the way into the heart of God. David says, "Purge me with hyssop,
and I shall be clean: wash me, and I shall be whiter than snow." It is
the application of the death of Christ to the life.

CRY FOR CLEANSING AND COMMUNION

Notice now David's cry for cleansing and communion.

> **Hide thy face from my sins, and blot out all mine iniqui-
> ties [Ps. 51:9].**

Blot out—David needed a spot remover. In getting ready to make an
extensive trip, every little book and folder I read advised, "Be sure to
take along a spot remover because you are going to get gravy on your
suit." How in the world did they know me? But I appreciate their ad-
vice because I know I'll need a spot remover. All of us do. David
needed a spot remover.

> **Create in me a clean heart, O God; and renew a right
> spirit within me [Ps. 51:10].**

The word for "create" here is the same word as in Genesis 1:1: "In the beginning God created the heaven and the earth"—*bara*, out of nothing. "I need a new heart," David said. "Create in me a *new* heart," and the word *create* means "out of nothing." In other words, there was nothing in David's heart that God could use. He was not asking for renovation or reformation. He was asking for something new. Sometimes we hear the invitation, "Give God your heart." May I ask you, "What do you think God wants with that old dirty, filthy heart of yours?" He doesn't want it. God is not asking anybody to give Him his heart. He wants to give you a *new* one. That's what He wants to do. "Create in me a new heart" is what David is asking for. "For we are his workmanship, created in Christ Jesus unto good works, which God hath before ordained that we should walk in them" (Eph. 2:10). "Therefore if any man be in Christ, he is a new creature: old things are passed away; behold, all things are become new" (2 Cor. 5:17). Let God give you a new heart.

David has another request:

Cast me not away from thy presence; and take not thy holy spirit from me [Ps. 51:11].

The spirit of God came upon David as king that he might be God's man. By the way, no Christian today can pray that prayer, because if you are indwelt by the Spirit of God, He will never leave you. You can grieve Him, you can quench Him, but you can never grieve Him away or quench Him away. We are told, "And grieve not the holy Spirit of God, whereby ye are sealed *unto the day of redemption*" (Eph. 4:30). Therefore no child of God can lose the Spirit of God. However, the Holy Spirit can be inoperative in a Christian's life, and that is what happened to David. He is asking that the Spirit of God may continue to work in his life.

Then he says,

Restore unto me the joy of thy salvation; and uphold me with thy free spirit [Ps. 51:12].

David did not lose his salvation. He lost the *joy* of his salvation, and he wanted communion with God restored. For he found out, as the prodigal son found out, that there is not nearly as much fun in the far country as there is in the Father's house.

He wanted all this for a purpose:

Then will I teach transgressors thy ways; and sinners shall be converted unto thee.

O LORD, open thou my lips; and my mouth shall shew forth thy praise [Ps. 51:13,15].

He wanted to praise God again.

Then shalt thou be pleased with the sacrifices of righteousness, with burnt offering and whole burnt offering: then shall they offer bullocks upon thine altar [Ps. 51:19].

He not only wanted to praise God, he wanted to please God.

The Lord Jesus went to dinner in the home of a Pharisee. A woman who had been saved came in there from the street. But Simon the Pharisee only knew her in the past, and he would have passed by on the other side rather than meet her on the street. But according to the custom of the day, when he had guests she had a right to come into his house and even stand and observe. She got to the place where our Lord was reclining (they used couches rather than chairs in that day), and she stood at His feet behind Him, weeping. She washed His feet with her tears, and wiped them with the hair of her head, and kissed His feet, and anointed them with ointment. Simon, His host, became critical. He began to find fault. And our Lord really rebuked him. He said, "When I came here you didn't even furnish me water to wash my feet. You didn't even extend to me the common courtesies. But this woman has not ceased to wash my feet with her tears. *She's* been forgiven. You have not" (Luke 7:44, paraphrase mine). Then He said to him, ". . . Her sins, which are many, are forgiven; for she loved much:

but to whom little is forgiven, the same loveth little" (Luke 7:47). We think we are all right. My friend, God cannot clear the guilty, and He says you and I are *guilty* before Him. The only way he could save you and me is to give His Son to die. For the worst sinner in the world that is all that is needed. And this is the way you and I are saved also. ". . . To whom little is forgiven, the same loveth little." To whom much is forgiven—oh, he loves much.

What is the measure of *your* love? Well, it is your estimate of your own sins. Is it possible that you do not confess your sins? When was the last time you wept over your sins? When was the last time you cried out in the night because of your failures? Thank God, there is forgiveness with Him. But there needs to be confession on our part.

PSALM 52

THEME: Antichrist, the mighty man of mischief

Psalm 52 begins a series of four psalms (52—55) which give a prophetic picture we get nowhere else of the coming Antichrist, the Man of Sin, who will be a world dictator and dominate Israel during the Tribulation. Our Lord referred to him in the Olivet discourse. The prophet Daniel and the apostle Paul both speak of him.

These four psalms are *maschil*, or instruction, psalms. They give us deep spiritual truths concerning the future. Many wild things are being said today in the field of prophecy. There is fanaticism in the great department of eschatology, the doctrine of future things; and some things are being said that should not be said. Because of the anxiety and uncertainty of this day and age in which we live, many folk are turning to the Word of God. Prophetic conferences are springing up everywhere, sponsored by churches that never before were interested in prophecy. Many speakers are attempting to be sensational by making prophetic statements that have no foundation in the Word of God.

This cluster of four psalms gives us accurate instructions relative to this "Man of Sin," the Antichrist who is coming.

Let me remind you that the superscription of the psalm is inspired; it is part of the psalm itself. It was written, "To the chief Musician, Maschil, A Psalm of David, when Doeg the Edomite came and told Saul, and said unto him, David is come to the house of Ahimelech." In other words, here is a man who betrayed David. David was hurt and betrayed by many men who professed to be his friends. We will see one of them in this particular section.

Boasting is a mark of the Antichrist.

Why boastest thou thyself in mischief, O mighty man?
the goodness of God endureth continually [Ps. 52:1].

Here is a man who is boasting of his *sin*. When David sinned, he kept quiet because he was under deep conviction. When the man of the world sins, he loves it and boasts about it. A mark of the Antichrist is that he will brag about his sin. This is the big difference between the child of God and the child of the devil. The child of God may sin just like the man in the world, because they both have an old nature. The difference is that the man of God will not boast about it. He will hang his head in shame. He will hate himself. But the sinner brags about what he does, and the Man of Sin, the Antichrist, will be the epitome of that type of man. And all the sinners will love him for it, you see.

> **Thy tongue deviseth mischiefs; like a sharp razor, working deceitfully [Ps. 52:2].**

God will tolerate the Man of Sin for a short period of time. For seven years the Antichrist's tongue will devise mischief.

> **Thou lovest evil more than good; and lying rather than to speak righteousness. Selah [Ps. 52:3].**

You have heard it said of some people that they would rather tell a lie even when it would have been easier to tell the truth. That will be true of the Antichrist.

> **Thou lovest all devouring words, O thou deceitful tongue [Ps. 52:4].**

This psalm has given us two names for the Man of Sin. In Psalm 52:1 he is called "mighty man." In this verse he is called a "deceitful tongue." You will not be able to believe a word he says. This is another one of his characteristics.

> **God shall likewise destroy thee for ever, he shall take thee away, and pluck thee out of thy dwelling place, and root thee out of the land of the living. Selah [Ps. 52:5].**

The word *destroy* means "to beat down." The Antichrist will be a world dictator whom no one can stop, no one except God. When the Lord Jesus Christ returns to earth, He will beat down the Man of Sin.

The righteous also shall see, and fear, and shall laugh at him [Ps. 52:6].

When God brings the Antichrist into judgment, when He beats him down, and the one whom the peoples of the earth once feared will be laughed at, the Antichrist will be the laughingstock of the universe.

Lo, this is the man that made not God his strength; but trusted in the abundance of his riches, and strengthened himself in his wickedness [Ps. 52:7].

He will be a very rich man. Our country has come to the place where only a rich man can win an election to office. The politicians talk a great deal about Abraham Lincoln, but I doubt if he would be able to make it to the presidency in this day. The Antichrist will be able to make it to the top at the beginning because he will be a rich man.

In the midst of this, the child of God will be able to say:

But I am like a green olive tree in the house of God: I trust in the mercy of God for ever and ever.

I will praise thee for ever, because thou hast done it: and I will wait on thy name; for it is good before thy saints [Ps. 52:8–9].

This brief psalm gives us a prophetic picture of the Antichrist and of the believing remnant who will suffer under his persecution, then will worship and praise God when he is dethroned.

PSALM 53

THEME: The fool, foreshadowing Antichrist, denies the existence of God

This psalm is the same as Psalm 14 as far as the translation is concerned, but there is something very interesting about it. It begins:

The fool hath said in his heart, There is no God. Corrupt are they, and have done abominable iniquity: there is none that doeth good [Ps. 53:1].

This psalm is "To the chief Musician upon Mahalath, Maschil, A Psalm of David." Mahalath has to do with sickness and sorrow, and it corresponds to the mournful condition of the last days when Antichrist is the ruler. He, of course, will be an atheist. The difference between Psalm 14 and Psalm 53 lies in the way the name of God is used. In Psalm 14 the name *Jehovah* is used four times and the name *Elohim* is used three times. Psalm 53 uses the name *Elohim* seven times. That is significant. Elohim is God's name as Creator. Now notice at what point atheism breaks through. It is relative to creation. The Bible, which is God's revelation, is denied and is no longer considered trustworthy, infallible, and inerrant. The first chapters of Genesis are branded as folklore and myth, even by some men who claim to be believers. Evolution is adopted as the explanation for the origin of all things. Many years ago an educator, who was president of one of the largest universities in this country, said, "We no longer take anything for granted, not even the existence of God." This is the spirit of the Antichrist. He will deny the existence of the Father and the Son. First John 2:22 tells us the mark of the Antichrist: "Who is a liar but he that denieth that Jesus is the Christ? He is antichrist, that denieth the Father and the Son."

If you are going to come to God, you will have to come by faith. "But without faith it is impossible to please him; for he that cometh to

God must believe that he is, and that he is a rewarder of them that diligently seek him" (Heb. 11:6). A number of years ago the Beatles (a rock music group) said, "We are more popular than Christ!" Of course that is not true now. Their popularity lasted for only a short time. It is interesting how the Lord Jesus Christ has moved back into the spotlight, having been out of it for so long.

Atheism is a characteristic of Antichrist. In the last days the forces of atheism will be headed up in him. Of him Paul wrote: "Who opposeth and exalteth himself above all that is called God, or that is worshipped; so that he as God sitteth in the temple of God, shewing himself that he is God" (2 Thess. 2:4).

This psalm ends with an expression of longing on the part of the believing remnant.

Oh that the salvation of Israel were come out of Zion! When God bringeth back the captivity of his people, Jacob shall rejoice, and Israel shall be glad [Ps. 53:6].

How can anyone say that God is through with the nation of Israel after reading this verse? "When God bringeth back the captivity of his people, Jacob shall rejoice, and Israel shall be glad." To deny that God has a future purpose for Israel is to deny the inerrancy and inspiration of Scripture. Yet men who say they are believers attempt to spiritualize this. A great company of Amillennialists (I studied in an amillennial seminary, and I know that crowd pretty well) have spiritualized the Book of Revelation instead of interpreting it literally. In my judgment, to spiritualize Scripture is practically to deny its inspiration. Now, my friend, God is not through with the nation of Israel. Listen to this verse again: "Oh that the salvation of Israel were come out of Zion! When God bringeth back the captivity of his people, Jacob shall rejoice, and Israel shall be glad." I think that even a child could understand what is being said here—that "Zion" means Zion, "Jacob" means Jacob, "Israel" means Israel, and "God" means God. This verse means exactly what it says. And God will answer this prayer. He will again deal with Israel as a nation.

PSALM 54

THEME: *A cry of faith in the time of Antichrist*

This marvelous little psalm is wedged in here, in the midst of all the troubles of the Great Tribulation, so that we can hear the cry of faith on the part of the remnant of God's people and of a great company of Gentiles, too.

Now note the historical background: "To the chief Musician on Neginoth, Maschil, A Psalm of David, when the Ziphims came and said to Saul, Doth not David hide himself with us?" From this introduction we discover several things. The neginoth was a stringed musical instrument. *Maschil* means that this is another psalm of instruction, a psalm of David. The Ziphims absolutely betrayed David. The Ziphims are also called Ziphites, and the record of their betrayal is found in 1 Samuel 23. When David learned that these people had told Saul where he was, he cried:

> **Save me, O God, by thy name, and judge me by thy strength.**
>
> **Hear my prayer, O God; give ear to the words of my mouth [Ps. 54:1-2].**

David was betrayed. And we are told that in the Great Tribulation period brother will betray brother. It will be a time again of awful betrayal.

It was a godless crowd that betrayed David. During the Tribulation period the godless Antichrist will be in power, and the Jewish remnant will suffer greatly under this Man of Sin.

> **For strangers are risen up against me, and oppressors seek after my soul: they have not set God before them. Selah [Ps. 54:3].**

David was in deep distress, as will be the remnant during the Tribulation of the future.

This brief psalm concludes with an expression of confidence in the help of God.

> **Behold, God is mine helper: the Lord is with them that uphold my soul.**
>
> **He shall reward evil unto mine enemies: cut them off in thy truth.**
>
> **I will freely sacrifice unto thee: I will praise thy name, O LORD; for it is good.**
>
> **For he hath delivered me out of all trouble: and mine eye hath seen his desire upon mine enemies [Ps. 54:4–7].**

We know from the historical record that God did deliver David from the treacherous Ziphites, and the faithful remnant can rest in the confidence that God will deliver them also. God will surely keep His promises.

PSALM 55

THEME: The darkest days under Antichrist

This psalm concludes this little cluster of four prophetic psalms that picture the Antichrist. Notice that this is another maschil psalm, which is a psalm of instruction. It pictures what I believe to be the darkest moment of the Tribulation period. The Antichrist, the Man of Sin, is fully portrayed here in a remarkable way, a way that many who are even students of prophecy have never considered.

This psalm is inscribed "To the chief Musician on Neginoth, Maschil, A Psalm of David." We are not told the exact background of this psalm, but I think we can make an educated guess. You will recall that David's own son, Absalom, led a rebellion against him. David was forced to leave Jerusalem. He found that many people were following his son, and he knew there would be trouble. In order that Jerusalem, his beloved city, would not be destroyed, he left it. He went back to the caves of the earth to hide. As David left his city, weeping, word was brought to him that Ahithophel, a member of his cabinet and close friend, had gone over to Absalom's side. He had betrayed David. We are told in 2 Samuel 15:30–31, "And David went up by the ascent of mount Olivet, and wept as he went up, and had his head covered, and he went barefoot: and all the people that was with him covered every man his head, and they went up, weeping as they went up. And one told David, saying, Ahithophel is among the conspiritors with Absalom. And David said, O LORD, I pray thee, turn the counsel of Ahithophel into foolishness." And that is exactly what God did— He turned the counsel of Ahithophel into foolishness. Keep these things in mind as we hit the high points of this psalm.

> **Give ear to my prayer, O God; and hide not thyself from my supplication.**
>
> **Attend unto me, and hear me: I mourn in my complaint, and make a noise [Ps. 55:1–2].**

David is like the squeaking wheel that gets the grease. David says, "I am making a noise to Thee, Lord. I am crying out to Thee because I am in a desperate situation. I have been betrayed by a friend."

> **Because of the voice of the enemy, because of the oppression of the wicked: for they cast iniquity upon me, and in wrath they hate me.**
>
> **My heart is sore pained within me: and the terrors of death are fallen upon me [Ps. 55:3–4].**

David did not know but what he would be slain at that time, especially when those who had been so close to him had deserted him.

> **And I said, Oh that I had wings like a dove! for then would I fly away, and be at rest [Ps. 55:6].**

At first, David was advised to fly away to his mountain, but he would not do it then. But now all seems lost. Even Ahithophel, his trusted advisor, has betrayed him. Does that remind you of something? It reminds me of Judas Iscariot who betrayed Christ. Also, it foreshadows the time when the nation will be betrayed by Antichrist.

Many of us have had the bitter experience of betrayal. I was a pastor for many years, and during those years I have had some wonderful people on my staff; but one or two of them have turned out to be like Ahithophel and Judas Iscariot. They betrayed me. When someone in whom you have placed your confidence betrays you, it hurts.

> **But it was thou, a man mine equal, my guide, and mine acquaintance [Ps. 55:13].**

David is speaking, I believe, of his "familiar friend," Ahithophel. This is also a picture of the Antichrist who will betray the nation of Israel. He will pretend to be their friend, will make a covenant with them and then will betray them.

> We took sweet counsel together, and walked unto the
> house of God in company [Ps. 55:14].

These are people who will pray with you and who will pray for you when you are with them. But when your back is turned, they will put a knife in it. There are people like that all around us. And if the Antichrist appeared tomorrow, he would have a following before the sun went down.

What David says next is imprecatory, I grant you, but listen to him:

> Let death seize upon them, and let them go down quick
> into hell: for wickedness is in their dwellings, and
> among them [Ps. 55:15].

"Let them go down quick into hell" is literally, "Let them go alive down to Sheol!" In our contemporary society we often hear the frightful expression, *Go to hell.* That is an awful thing to say, and David almost said that relative to Ahithophel. In contrast to him, our Lord Jesus prayed for them who despitefully used Him and instructed us to do likewise.

> As for me, I will call upon God; and the LORD shall save
> me.
>
> Evening, and morning, and at noon, will I pray, and cry
> aloud: and he shall hear my voice [Ps. 55:16–17].

What a picture that gives of David's distress—"Evening, and morning, and at noon, will I pray, and cry aloud." My friend, one good thing your enemy will do for you is to cause you to pray more than you have ever prayed before!

Now notice this picture of Antichrist—oh, is he a liar! Remember that the Lord Jesus said the devil was a liar from the beginning (John 8:44), and Antichrist is right out of the pit of hell.

> **The words of his mouth were smoother than butter, but war was in his heart: his words were softer than oil, yet were they drawn swords [Ps. 55:21].**

Ahithophel, pretending to be a friend to David, was plotting against him. He was a little adumbration of Antichrist.

> **Cast thy burden upon the LORD, and he shall sustain thee: he shall never suffer the righteous to be moved [Ps. 55:22].**

Dear Christian friend, let me say to you: Turn your enemies over to God. "Dearly beloved, avenge not yourselves, but rather give place unto wrath: for it is written, Vengeance is mine; I will repay, saith the Lord" (Rom. 12:19). Turn over those who would betray you to the Lord. I was a pastor for over forty years, and I feel I can speak about this subject with some experience and knowledge. I have found that the Lord does a better job in dealing with my enemies than I can. He knows just *how* to do it. Cast your burden upon the Lord and He will take care of everything. During the days of the Great Tribulation, Israel will finally turn to the Lord because there will be no place else for them to turn.

> **But thou, O God, shalt bring them down into the pit of destruction: bloody and deceitful men shall not live out half their days; but I will trust in thee [Ps. 55:23].**

What about you today? What about me? How are we going to live in the world today? Are we going to hate people and criticize them for what they do to us? Are we going to cry when we are betrayed and wronged? No! Let's start trusting in the Lord. That's the way out.

PSALM 56

THEME: David's fear and trust

This psalm brings us to another delightful cluster of psalms (56—60) known as the michtam psalms. What does *michtam* mean? It speaks of that which is substantial, or enduring, or fixed. *Michtam* literally means "engraven" or "permanent." This word pictures that which is unmoveable, steadfast, stable and enduring. In Psalm 57:7 when David says, "My heart is fixed," that is a *michtam*.

Delitzsch called Psalm 56 "the cheerful courage of a fugitive." You will recall that in Psalm 55 David wished that he had the wings of a dove so that he could fly away and lodge in the wilderness (Ps. 55:6–7); in this psalm his desire is realized. The enemy is outside. However, David is in great danger; the wicked are on every side. But through it all God delivered him. The historical background of this psalm has to do with the Philistines capturing David at Gath. David's experience is a picture of the Great Tribulation period. All of these psalms have a prophetic undertone. Between the historical (David's experiences) and the prophetical (Israel's experience in the future), is a real message for us today. All of the Psalms have a message for our own hearts.

This psalm is inscribed "To the chief Musician upon Jonathelem-rechokim, Michtam of David, when the Philistines took him in Gath."

> **Be merciful unto me, O God: for man would swallow me up; he fighting daily oppresseth me.**
>
> **Mine enemies would daily swallow me up: for they be many that fight against me, O thou most High [Ps. 56:1–2].**

Now let me give you Dr. Gaebelein's translation of these verses—he was a Hebrew scholar. "Be gracious unto me, O God, for man would swallow me up; throughout the day fighting he oppresseth me. They are watching me and would swallow me up the whole day; for many are they that fight against me in pride" (*The Book of Psalms*, p. 232). David is surrounded by the enemy. He seems to be on a hot seat. What is he going to do in a bad spot like this?

What time I am afraid, I will trust in thee [Ps. 56:3].

Was David afraid? He certainly was. A couple heard me make the statement that when I travel by plane I do not enjoy the trip because there is fear in my heart. They thought there was something wrong with my faith in God. My friend, fear will bring out *faith* in your life. Listen to David, "What time I am afraid, I will trust in thee." These people who sit back comfortably and say, "I haven't any fear," may mean that they are insensitive to the circumstances and problems that really exist. Or they may have a foolish sort of faith. David admitted he was afraid, but he *trusted* the Lord to take care of him.

Can you have fear and faith at the same time? The Scripture says, "There is no fear in love; but perfect love casteth out fear: because fear hath torment. He that feareth is not made perfect in love" (1 John 4:18). Perfect love casts out fear. *Love* will do it. But you can have faith and still be afraid. I hope this will comfort some folks, because there are many foolish things being said which are not scriptural.

Thou tellest my wanderings: put thou my tears into thy bottle: are they not in thy book? [Ps. 56:8].

"The Lord counts my wanderings." The Lord knows about every trip you take and about every trip I take. I have thought about this many times while I have been studying the Psalms. Since I have been retired, I have gone from place to place for speaking engagements. Sometimes I ask my wife, "What did I speak about when we were in a certain place in Florida, or when we were in Texas, Washington, or the Hawaiian Islands?" I had forgotten, but the Lord has written all of that down. If I just had access to His book, it would be a great help.

"My tears have been put into thy bottle." A note in *The New Scofield Bible* concerning this subject says, "Sometimes, in olden days in the East, mourners would catch their tears in bottles (water skins) and place them at the tombs of their loved ones"—to show how much they had grieved. Let me add to that something John Bunyan, the tinker of Bedford, said, "God preserves our tears in a bottle, so that He can wipe them away." When I read that, I wished I had cried more. We need to weep more. Matthew Henry said, "The tears of God's persecuted people are bottled up, and sealed among God's treasures."

In God will I praise his word: in the LORD will I praise his word [Ps. 56:10].

Someone wrote to me and said, "You make too much of the Bible. You are everlastingly talking about the Word of God." That is what David did also. There are so few people who are praising His Word that I am going to try to make up for them.

In God have I put my trust: I will not be afraid what man can do unto me [Ps. 56:11].

How wonderful it is to have a resource and a recourse to God.

For thou hast delivered my soul from death: wilt not thou deliver my feet from falling, that I may walk before God in the light of the living? [Ps. 56:13].

David said, especially after his great sin, "I want to walk before God so that I won't slip up again." As far as the record is concerned, he did not slip up again, either. The king of Babylon committed that kind of sin every day of the year; it was commonplace for him. But it was not the practice of David. He said, "I want to walk before God." Today we are enjoined to walk in the Holy Spirit. ". . . Walk in the Spirit, and ye shall not fulfil the lust of the flesh" (Gal. 5:16). God has given us more than a walking stick. He has given us the indwelling Holy Spirit. To walk in the Spirit means to utterly and absolutely depend on the Spirit of God. This gets right down to where the rubber meets the road. As we will see in our study of Galatians, we are to get down from our highchairs and start walking. We learn to walk in the Spirit as we learned to walk physically, by trying it. Of course we will fail time and time again, but we are to get up, dust ourselves off, and start out again. You will learn to walk in the Spirit if you *keep at* it and commit yourself to Him every day.

PSALM 57

THEME: A cry for mercy

This is the second michtam psalm, and it has an added title—*Al-taschith*, meaning "destroy not." As we get into this psalm we will see that it has real meaning. It is inscribed "To the chief Musician, Al-taschith, Michtam of David, when he fled from Saul in the cave."

David spent time in the caves along the Dead Sea by Engedi. It is below sea level and a hot spot during the summer; in the winter it is a delightful place. It is rugged country. The cave of Adullam is in that area also. It is the belief of many expositors that this psalm has reference to that cave of Adullam where David meditated on many of the psalms that he composed. In them we see that his sufferings foreshadowed the sufferings of Christ and those of the godly remnant during the time of Jacob's trouble. Also these psalms speak to us today, which is the wonder of the Word of God.

> Be merciful unto me, O God, be merciful unto me: for my soul trusteth in thee: yea, in the shadow of thy wings will I make my refuge, until these calamities be overpast [Ps. 57:1].

I don't know about you, but my prayer is the same as David's, "O God be merciful to me." I want God to be merciful to me. I don't want Him to be just with me and righteous. If He is, I am going to get a whipping. I want Him to be merciful and gracious to me. He is that kind of a God—rich in mercy. He has enough for me—and I am going to require a lot of it—but there will be enough for you also.

"In the shadow of thy wings will I make my refuge"—or as Dr. Gaebelein has it, "in the shadow of Thy wings will I find shelter." David experienced this shelter. The nation of Israel did not, however.

In Matthew 23:37 the Lord Jesus said, "O Jerusalem, Jerusalem, thou that killest the prophets, and stonest them which are sent unto thee, how often would I have gathered thy children together, even as a hen gathereth her chickens under her wings, and ye would not!" Israel has not as yet come under His wings. Are you ready to come under His wings? In other words, be obedient to Him, to love Him—Jesus said, "If ye love me, keep my commandments" (John 14:15)—and to walk in the Spirit?

Now notice these wonderful statements:

> **He shall send from heaven, and save me from the re-
> proach of him that would swallow me up. Selah. God
> shall send forth his mercy and his truth [Ps. 57:3].**

This will be literally fulfilled for the faithful remnant when Christ returns in power and great glory; and they will say, ". . . Lo, this is our God; we have waited for him, and he will save us: this is the Lord; we have waited for him, we will be glad and rejoice in his salvation" (Isa. 25:9).

> **My soul is among lions: and I lie even among them that
> are set on fire, even the sons of men, whose teeth are
> spears and arrows, and their tongue a sharp sword [Ps.
> 57:4].**

Satan goes up and down this world like a roaring lion seeking whom he may devour (1 Peter 5:8), and he has a lot of little lions helping him, by the way.

Remember that these michtam psalms have to do with that which is permanent and enduring, that which is substantial and lasting.

> **My heart is fixed, O God, my heart is fixed: I will sing
> and give praise [Ps. 57:7].**

Then notice this beautiful expression:

Awake up, my glory; awake, psaltery and harp: I myself will awake early [Ps. 57:8].

"I will wake the morning dawn" is Dr. Gaebelein's translation. What a beautiful expression! The night of sin and suffering is over. Satan's rule is finished, and the morning has come. The Sun of Righteousness has risen with healing in His wings. How wonderful! What assurance we find in this psalm.

PSALM 58

THEME: An imprecatory prayer against the enemy

Notice that this is another *al-taschith* as well as another michtam psalm. It means that there is something substantial and enduring here, and it means "destroy not."

Now it begins with a question, and who is asking it? I believe it is God who is speaking, using the pen of David.

> **Do ye indeed speak righteousness, O congregation? do**
> **ye judge uprightly, O ye sons of men? [Ps. 58:1].**

Or, as Dr. Gaebelein translates it: "Is righteousness indeed silent? Do ye judges speak it? Do ye with uprightness judge the children of men?"

The day is going to come when the Lord is going to call on the judges to turn in their report. God is asking, "Is righteousness indeed silent? Do ye judges speak it?" They will have to answer these questions.

This is another imprecatory prayer. David's enemies are all around him.

> **The wicked are estranged from the womb: they go**
> **astray as soon as they be born, speaking lies.**
>
> **Their poison is like the poison of a serpent: they are like**
> **the deaf adder that stoppeth her ear;**
>
> **Which will not hearken to the voice of charmers,**
> **charming never so wisely.**
>
> **Break their teeth, O God, in their mouth: break out the**
> **great teeth of the young lions, O LORD [Ps. 58:3–6].**

David prays for six destructions to come upon his enemies in this psalm: (1) "Break out the great teeth of the young lions." We have already found that the enemy is like a lion. There are those who say that a Christian cannot pray this way. I have prayed that the Lord would absolutely deal with Satan. He is like a roaring lion, and I hope God breaks his teeth. I don't consider that unchristian at all. David is speaking of his enemies, and he is under law; so he is asking for justice.

Now he uses another figure of speech:

> Let them melt away as waters which run continually:
> when he bendeth his bow to shoot his arrows, let them
> be as cut in pieces [Ps. 58:7].

(2) Wickedness was like a flood! He asks that this flood of wickedness might just melt away. (3) "When he bendeth his bow to shoot his arrows, let them be as cut in pieces." The enemy is like a marksman who is shooting at him. What a picture we have here!

> As a snail which melteth, let every one of them pass
> away: like the untimely birth of a woman, that they may
> not see the sun [Ps. 58:8].

(4) "As a snail which melteth, let every one of them pass away." There is a certain snail in that country called a "slimeworm" which actually melts away in the heat of the sun. David is saying, "The enemy leaves a slimy trail, but evaporate him! Get rid of that slimy trail through the world." (5) "Like the untimely birth of a woman, that they may not see the sun." That is, may they not come to fruition in the things they plan in the evil womb of their mind. May it come to nought.

> Before your pots can feel the thorns, he shall take them
> away as with a whirlwind, both living, and in his wrath
> [Ps. 58:9].

(6) "Before your pots can feel the thorns, he shall take them away"—
the twigs of the bramble bush are gathered together and put under the
pot to heat it, then a wind comes along and blows them away. David
says, "Oh, God, remove them before they can do their dirty work,
before they can burn and sear."

This is a tremendous prayer.

PSALMS 59 AND 60

THEME: God's people surrounded by enemies

Psalm 59 is closely linked with the two preceding psalms. It is also an *al-taschith* ("destroy not") and a michtam of David. Again in this psalm we see David surrounded by his enemies, and prophetically it describes the suffering remnant during the Tribulation, surrounded by enemies.

The inspired title of this psalm places it at the time Saul sent messengers, and they watched the house to kill him. The historical record is found in 1 Samuel 19.

> Deliver me from mine enemies, O my God: defend me from them that rise up against me.
>
> Deliver me from the workers of iniquity, and save me from bloody men.
>
> For, lo, they lie in wait for my soul: the mighty are gathered against me; not for my transgression, nor for my sin, O LORD [Ps. 59:1–3].

As is typical with David's psalms, it concludes with an expression of faith and trust in God's deliverance.

> But I will sing of thy power; yea, I will sing aloud of thy mercy in the morning: for thou hast been my defence and refuge in the day of my trouble.
>
> Unto thee, O my strength, will I sing: for God is my defence, and the God of my mercy [Ps. 59:16–17].

In the case of David, God did deliver him. My friend, God will not forsake those who are His own. The believing remnant of Israel will be

delivered by the coming of Christ Himself, and He will judge the nations of the world.

Psalm 60 is the last of these michtam psalms and describes the
time David was victorious over his enemies the Edomites. The Edomites were soundly defeated and never rallied after it.

Prophetically it is the picture of the deliverance God will give to
His people, the remnant of Israel, after the suffering of the Great Tribulation.

> **O God, thou hast cast off, thou hast scattered us, thou
> hast been displeased; O turn thyself to us again [Ps.
> 60:1].**

Now here is the answer:

> **God hath spoken in his holiness; I will rejoice, I will
> divide Shechem, and mete out the valley of Succoth [Ps.
> 60:6].**

And how will it be accomplished?

> **Who will bring me into the strong city? who will lead
> me into Edom? [Ps. 60:9].**

"Who will bring me into the strong [or the fortified] city?" That is the
question; now notice the answer.

> **Wilt not thou, O God, which hadst cast us off? and thou,
> O God, which didst not go out with our armies? [Ps.
> 60:10].**

God will restore His saints. In any age He will restore them—though
they be in trouble and difficulty and even sin. My, isn't God good!

PSALM 61

THEME: Cry and confidence of the godly

The theme throughout this new cluster of psalms (61—68) is the cry and confidence of the godly. As you listen to the pleadings of the godly in these eight psalms, you will find beautifully described their steadfast confidence in the Lord. You will also see the Lord Jesus Christ in these psalms, as well as derive great help for yourself. Psalm 61 is "To the chief Musician upon Neginah, A Psalm of David." This is a psalm that you can play with a stringed instrument and would be appropriate for a guitar, because of the mournful undertone. It is a prayer from David's heart. This makes it different from the modern prayers we so often hear, which make our prayer meetings so stereotyped. All many of us do is turn in to the Lord a grocery list of the things we want. We ask Him to take them down off the shelf and give them to us so we won't have to go through the checkout stand and pay for them. I think that attitude has killed prayer today. I believe in the organization, the mechanics, and the arrangement of prayer, but I also believe prayer should come from the *heart*. You seldom hear that deep heart cry in prayer any more, but you will find it in David's prayer.

Hear my cry, O God; attend unto my prayer.

From the end of the earth will I cry unto thee, when my heart is overwhelmed: lead me to the rock that is higher than I [Ps. 61:1–2].

David says, "From the end of the earth will I call upon thee." When you pray, have you ever felt that God is way up in the heavens and you are way down here? David feels that he is at the end of the earth and God is way off yonder. He is trying to get closer. He wants to get to a Rock that is higher than he is. The reason I am opposed to this modern viewpoint of Jesus is because the Jesus who is presented is not a

superstar at all. He is just a man like I am. He is a rock that is no higher
than I am. I need to be led to the Rock that is higher than I. The Word
of God tells me that that Rock is Jesus Christ (1 Cor. 10:4), and He is a
lot higher than I am! What a picture we have here of the Lord!

> **For thou hast been a shelter for me, and a strong tower**
> **from the enemy [Ps. 61:3].**

What a comforting picture of God! He is a *shelter* from storms. He is a
strong *tower* to protect us from our enemies.

> **I will abide in thy tabernacle for ever: I will trust in the**
> **covert of thy wings. Selah [Ps. 61:4].**

Once again the word *wings* is mentioned in connection with God. The
Lord Jesus also used this illustration when He spoke of gathering Jerusalem to Himself as a mother hen gathers her little ones under her
wings to protect them.

> **For thou, O God, hast heard my vows: thou hast given**
> **me the heritage of those that fear thy name [Ps. 61:5].**

David made vows; he promised God something. We *ask* things of
God. Did you ever promise Him anything? (I have promised more
than I have delivered, I know that.) You go to God continually and ask
Him for something. Why don't you promise to do something for Him?
David did, and God heard his vow.

> **Thou wilt prolong the king's life: and his years as many**
> **generations.**
>
> **He shall abide before God for ever: O prepare mercy and**
> **truth, which may preserve him [Ps. 61:6–7].**

Here he goes again asking for mercy. David needed the mercy of God. I
believe that the closer we get to God, the more we realize that we can't

bring Him down to our level, but we will see Him high and lifted up. Then we will be in the same position as Isaiah was when he had a vision of the Lord sitting upon His throne. We will recognize our uncleanness and our need of His mercy.

So will I sing praise unto thy name for ever, that I may daily perform my vows [Ps. 61:8].

Make your vows and then get close to God. Sing His praises, and He will help you fulfill your vows.

PSALM 62

THEME: The only psalm

This is called the "only" psalm, not because there are no others—there are 149 others—but because the word *only* is significant. "Truly [better translated *only*] my soul waiteth upon God . . . He *only* is my rock and my salvation . . . they *only* consult to cast him down . . .wait thou *only* upon God . . . He *only* is my rock."

The superscription here is "To the chief Musician, to Jeduthun, A Psalm of David." Psalm 39 was also written to Jeduthun. He was one of the chief musicians. His name is mentioned several times in the Psalms. Apparently he led the orchestra and the choir when this psalm was used.

This is a simple psalm. It is one of simple faith. It reveals a faith and confidence in God that is akin to a child's faith in his parents.

Perowne gives us a wonderful statement concerning this psalm: "Scarcely anywhere do we find faith in God more nobly asserted, more victoriously triumphant; the vanity of man, of human strength and riches, more clearly confessed; courage in the midst of peril more calm and more unshaken, than in this Psalm, which is as forcible in its conception, and its language, as it is remarkable for the vigorous and cheerful piety it breathes" *(The Book of Psalms,* Vol. I, p. 442). Although the inspired text does not give us this information, tradition tells us that this psalm came from the greatest heartbreak of David's life—the rebellion led by his son Absalom.

We turn to the historical record, and read this language: "And David went up by the ascent of mount Olivet, and wept as he went up, and had his head covered, and he went barefoot: and all the people that was with him covered every man his head, and they went up, weeping as they went up" (2 Sam. 15:30). That was a tragic time in the life of David. It was his dramatic moment, his time of crisis. Thomas Paine spoke of times that try men's souls. This time had come to the old king.

Absalom, David's son, is marching into Jerusalem. His entry is forcing a time of decision. There are some who are choosing David; others are choosing Absalom. It is a time when David has found who are the loyal and disloyal in the ranks. The betrayers and followers are well-marked. An important man is Ahithophel (related by marriage through Bathsheba to David), an astute statesman, a man of sagacity, of wonderful ability, a counselor upon whom David had leaned. Ahithophel has deserted and gone over to Absalom. It was a great grief to David when he found that this trusted man had deserted him. Then Ziba, the servant of Mephibosheth, came and said that his master, the son of Jonathan, whom David had befriended, had also betrayed him.

As David fled from the city, barefoot and weeping, there stood Shimei, a Benjamite, still loyal to former King Saul. From a heart of bitter hatred for David, he threw stones and heaped cursings upon the old king as he fled.

We see Absalom entering Jerusalem in triumph, and the same crowd that once shouted to the rafters for David is now shouting deliriously for Absalom. Centuries later the children of these people were the ones who shouted "Hosanna" to the Lord Jesus Christ, and shortly after cried, "Crucify him." David knew the sting of the voice of the mob, and Psalm 62 is the song of David in that hour of ignominy.

Here we find a man who has committed his way to God, one who is traveling in the spiritual stratosphere; a man who is living above the storms, shocks, and stresses of this life. And as we read this psalm which comes from his heart in this hour of darkness, this time of testing, this hour of defeat, we are amazed to find not one note of discouragement, nor suggestion of fear, nor word of distress. There is neither rancor nor bitterness welling up in the heart of the psalmist. He sings forth a song of salvation, a paean of praise, an opus of optimism. It is a song of sanguinity, a thesis of trust, and a work of wonder. How could David write such a Hallelujah chorus out of an experience so dark?

THE TEST OF FAITH

Truly my soul waiteth upon God: from him cometh my salvation [Ps. 62:1].

No doubt there were those around David—fanatics of those days—
who urged that he stand his ground and thereby exhibit his faith, for
he was God's anointed and God should overrule this whole matter.
Not David! He said that his life was in God's hands, and it seemed best
that he leave. David lived above the hue and cry of little men. He did
not listen to pious shibboleths, for while little men cried for a miracle,
David avowed to walk in the dark, trusting God. O for a faith like that!
A God-given faith! What others called defeat, to David was but a test
of faith. David can retreat from Jerusalem, and it is still going to sound
like a victory.

> **He only is my rock and my salvation; he is my defence; I**
> **shall not be greatly moved [Ps. 62:2].**

Zadok, the high priest, is come out to go with David. He is faithful
and has brought the ark, a symbol to the Israelites of God's presence in
their midst, and he is following David when the old king turns and,
seeing the ark, commands Zadok to carry it back to the city, for ". . . if I
shall find favour in the eyes of the LORD, he will bring me again, and
shew me both it, and his habitation: But if he thus say, I have no delight in thee; behold, here am I, let him do to me as seemeth good unto
him" (2 Sam. 15:25–26).

If I can but make this great truth clear so that it will live for you!
Here is a man so wholly committed to God that he turns aside from
any thought of merit in the ark, clinging only unto God and saying to
Zadok that if it is God's will for him to come back to this city, he will
be allowed to come back; if not, then he is in God's hands. He refuses
to attempt to force God to do anything but determines to go the way
God leads, regardless of the path. O, to live like that today!

> **How long will ye imagine mischief against a man? ye**
> **shall be slain all of you: as a bowing wall shall ye be,**
> **and as a tottering fence [Ps. 62:3].**

David tells them that they are just running over him "as a bowing
wall . . . and as a tottering fence." He says, "How long will ye imagine

mischief against a man? ye shall be slain all of you." Here he is thinking of Ziba, servant of Mephibosheth, who did a dastardly thing,
thinking he would gain favor with David. He said his master had deserted, which was not true.

Then he thinks of Ahithophel, his best friend and wisest of his
counselors. Ahithophel went over to the other side in David's darkest
hour. Here in this psalm David is speaking of Ahithophel prophetically as Judas Iscariot. Ahithophel was in the inner circle and was the
man that David leaned upon.

David says that they are running over him as a mob runs over a
fence, but he says it is all right if it is God's will.

**They only consult to cast him down from his excellency:
they delight in lies: they bless with their mouth, but they
curse inwardly. Selah [Ps. 62:4].**

Let us understand David's action under the bitter attack of Shimei.
While David was on the throne, Shimei bowed like the rest of them;
but, when he was free to express his heart of hatred, we find him curs-
ing David and hurling rocks after him as he fled from Jerusalem.
David had a loyal captain by the name of Abishai, a son of Zeruiah,
who said to the king, ". . . Why should this dead dog curse my lord the
king? let me go over, I pray thee, and take off his head" (2 Sam. 16:9).

My friend, if you want an example of what the Scripture means by
". . . Vengeance is mine; I will repay, saith the Lord" (Rom. 12:19),
listen to David as he replies to his captain: "And the king said . . . so
let him curse, because the Lord hath said unto him, Curse David. Who
shall then say, Wherefore hast thou done so?" (2 Sam. 16:10). In other
words, David tells him "God has permitted him to curse me; you let
him curse me." Have you ever stopped to think, my friend, that God
has given you certain enemies for a definite purpose to test you that
you might become a better Christian? Do not become alarmed at the
presence of enemies and difficulties that God has permitted to cumber
your path. He is not bearing hard on you. Would that we would trust
God to the extent that we would not cry out at a time like that!

THE TIME OF FAITH

When is the time of faith? Is it on a sunshiny day when there is not a cloud in your sky? Is it a time when everything is going exactly right, with nothing to mar your outlook? David's answer is that the best time to trust God is at the crisis moment of your life—

My soul, wait thou only upon God; for my expectation is from him [Ps. 62:5].

This is a Bible definition of prayer.

I once had a little card sent to me bearing a message that seemed rather important, so I kept it. Here it is: "True prayer is the Holy Spirit speaking in the believer, through the Son, to the Father." That is prayer; it is real prayer. "My expectation is from him." David is saying here that he is not making some wild prayer, some audacious statement, that he is not demanding that God do anything—"My expectation is from him." David is expecting God to put into his heart the thing that He wants done; therefore, he will be praying for the thing that is best.

We wonder again if some pious person around David might not have suggested to him that he was in such a tight place that they should have a prayer meeting. To this David would have said to them that his whole life was a life of prayer, "My expectation is from him." Here is the illustration that Paul had in mind when he said, "Pray without ceasing" (1 Thess. 5:17). Now by this Paul did not mean that you are to get on your knees and remain there twenty-four hours a day. But Paul did mean for you to get on your knees and pray and then live in the expectation of that prayer for twenty-four hours every day. So David is not going to call a prayer meeting. In fact, the amazing thing is that this psalm has no prayer in it at all. But we find that the entire psalm is in the atmosphere of prayer. He is a man so committed to God that his life and actions are that of prayer.

Now we see this old king going out of Jerusalem; we hear him weeping. But these exterior things fade away when we glimpse the depths of his heart, for he is a man who is committed to God and he will go with God regardless of what the outcome might be. Other men would have become bitter, but not David. He is saying something here that is tremendous: "My soul, wait thou only upon God; . . . my expectation is from him."

He only is my rock and my salvation: he is my defence; I shall not be moved [Ps. 62:6].

That is the central truth of the psalm. That is the central truth of David's life. That is the dynamo that ran his life. That is the thing that caused him to stand head and shoulders above other men on the horizon of history. It has caused him to cast a long shadow down the corridor of time. "He only is my rock."

When we come to the New Testament, we can see what the Lord Jesus means when He says this tremendous thing: "And whosoever shall fall on this stone shall be broken: but on whomsoever it shall fall, it will grind him to powder" (Matt. 21:44). Christ is that Rock, that Stone. There is coming a day when the Stone cut out without hands will fall on this earth. Today, you and I can fall on this Stone, and those who fall on it will be saved.

A little Scottish woman got up in a testimony meeting and gave this as her testimony: "You know, sometimes I tremmel [tremble] on the rock, but the rock never tremmels under me." Are you on this Rock? Whosoever falls on this Rock shall be saved. This is what Paul meant when he said, "For other foundation can no man lay than that is laid, which is Jesus Christ" (1 Cor. 3:11). David said, "He only is my rock. He is the One I am trusting. O, the throne is toppling, Jerusalem is in convulsions, the people have turned against me, but I am on the Rock!" David has learned that glorious lesson.

In God is my salvation and my glory: the rock of my strength, and my refuge, is in God.

Trust in him at all times; ye people, pour out your heart before him: God is a refuge for us. Selah [Ps. 62:7–8].

This is a very personal psalm. Notice that God is "my salvation . . . my glory . . . my strength . . . my refuge."

THE TRIUMPH OF FAITH

Surely men of low degree are vanity, and men of high degree are a lie: to be laid in the balance, they are altogether lighter than vanity [Ps. 62:9].

He has learned that one cannot trust the mob, for they are fickle. He has found that men of high degree, such as Ahithophel, are not to be trusted. They cannot be leaned upon. And this is the first thing that a new Christian must learn—not to look to men but to God. Many new Christians have become discouraged, disappointed, and disillusioned, for they have their eyes set upon a man. A young Christian told me recently that he had gotten his eyes on a man, and it had all but made shipwreck of his faith. David knew all of the time that he could not trust men, so his faith was fixed utterly upon God. He rested upon a Rock that could not be moved.

Then he tells us that we cannot trust in material things either:

Trust not in oppression, and become not vain in robbery: if riches increase, set not your heart upon them [Ps. 62:10].

And now hear the conclusion: Why is it that you can trust God?

God hath spoken once; twice have I heard this; that power belongeth unto God [Ps. 62:11].

Friend, you can trust God because He can do anything that requires power. He has all power, and He can do anything he wants to do! Power did not reside in David. He was simply a great king because God made of him a great king. Now He has permitted men to force him to leave Jerusalem: and, if it is not God's will that he return, then he will not go back. But he is resigning all to God for He alone is the One who has *all* power.

The mad rush to gain power is the destroying element in the world at this hour. In the effort to gain power, the bomb has been created.

This form of power wreaks destruction. It is man's effort at power. But David says he has discovered that with real power there is another element that goes with it always:

Also unto thee, O Lord, belongeth mercy: for thou renderest to every man according to his work [Ps. 62:12].

If you have power, you ought to be able to exercise mercy. David is saying that his God who can exercise power is a God who can also exercise mercy. To Zadok he said that he wanted him to take back the mercy seat and place it in the temple, for he would find mercy with God.

At the very heart of Old Testament religion was the mercy seat. At the heart of the Christian faith today is mercy. "Come every soul by sin oppressed, there's mercy with the Lord." I think that is what Brother George Bennard meant when he wrote: "I'll cling to the old rugged cross." Mercy!

Friend, let me make a suggestion. This psalm simply states this precious relationship with God. David just pours out his heart to God. He talks to God and tells Him, "You are my salvation; You are my rock." So many people get uptight in a prayer meeting or in a church service. They feel oppression in prayer—they want to say the right things and use the right words. Public prayer is all right, but let me suggest that you go aside and be alone with God. Perhaps you can drive along in your car, or maybe you can find a good quiet corner in a room in your home. Find a place where you can be quiet before God. Then "take the lid off." There is a time to "gird up your loins," and there is a time to take off your girdle and just let yourself go before God. When I was in Pasadena, a ladies' group put a shaggy rug in my study. It was the first shaggy rug I ever had, and I liked it very much. I used to get down on that rug, on my face before God, and pour my heart out to Him. It did me good, and it will do you good. It is the best tonic you could have.

PSALM 63

THEME: Thirst for the Water of Life

This is "A Psalm of David, when he was in the wilderness of Judah." This is a special psalm. It is an ointment that is poured out upon all kinds of sores. It is a bandage for bruises. It is a balm to put upon wounds to help them heal. It has been a marvelous psalm for the church. It speaks of the thirst for the Water of Life. Chrysostom said that it was ordained and agreed upon by the primitive fathers that no day should pass without the public singing of this psalm, and in the primitive church this psalm was sung every morning or every time there was a public gathering. They always began the morning service with it.

This psalm is the expression of wonderful thoughts.

> **O God, thou art my God; early will I seek thee: my soul thirsteth for thee, my flesh longeth for thee in a dry and thirsty land, where no water is;**
>
> **To see thy power and thy glory, so as I have seen thee in the sanctuary [Ps. 63:1–2].**

These two verses were translated by Dr. Gaebelein thus: "O God, Thou art my God; early do I seek Thee; my soul thirsteth for Thee, my flesh pineth for Thee, in a dry, thirsty land without water; as I gazed upon Thee in the Sanctuary, to see Thy power and glory" *(The Book of Psalms, p. 251).* It is faith, and faith alone, that can speak like this. God, the Eternal One, transcends all human thinking. He is the Creator. He is the Redeemer. He is my Father. It was He whom David sought. He knew what it was to be thirsty. He had hidden in caves down by the Dead Sea, and it is some of the driest land I have ever seen. California, Arizona, and New Mexico haven't anything that can touch that dry land around Engedi. It is a place where you can get thirsty! If you are ever over there, make sure that you have water with you. David's soul thirsted for God. Do you feel that way about Him? Do you have a love for Him, or has He become a burden to you? Oh, that we might thirst for Him!

> **Thus will I bless thee while I live: I will lift up my hands in thy name.**

> **My soul shall be satisfied as with marrow and fatness; and my mouth shall praise thee with joyful lips [Ps. 63:4–5].**

David is saying that he would rather have fellowship with God than have a gourmet dinner.

> **When I remember thee upon my bed, and meditate on thee in the night watches.**

> **Because thou hast been my help, therefore in the shadow of thy wings will I rejoice [Ps. 63:6–7].**

David thought about God—meditated upon Him—during the night when he couldn't sleep. My friend, meditating upon God's goodness is a lot better than counting sheep!

> **My soul followeth hard after thee: thy right hand upholdeth me [Ps. 63:8].**

Oh, that our souls might follow hard after Him!

This is a great psalm. Remember, it is the psalm of the morning and was sung at every service of the early church. Maybe we can't sing it in our day—I don't know.

PSALM 64

THEME: The evil may win, but God will judge them

This psalm also has a historical background in the life of David, although we can't locate it exactly. Prophetically, it looks yonder in the future to the day when Israel will be in Great Tribulation and the godly remnant will use this psalm. Someone might say, "My, there certainly are a lot of psalms for the Day of Jacob's Trouble." Yes, there are, and the people are going to need every one of them. Also, this is a very fine psalm for you and me.

> **Hear my voice, O God, in my prayer: preserve my life from fear of the enemy.**
>
> **Hide me from the secret counsel of the wicked; from the insurrection of the workers of iniquity [Ps. 64:1–2].**

Once again, David is asking God to hide him. David prayed this kind of prayer time and time again. His refuge was prayer. It was the only refuge he had. Prayer is the only refuge Israel will have in that day of tribulation.

This brief psalm concludes with David expressing his confidence in God. His God was his only hope.

> **But God shall shoot at them with an arrow; suddenly shall they be wounded.**
>
> **So they shall make their own tongue to fall upon themselves: all that see them shall flee away.**
>
> **And all men shall fear, and shall declare the work of God; for they shall wisely consider of his doing.**
>
> **The righteous shall be glad in the Lord, and shall trust in him; and all the upright in heart shall glory [Ps. 64:7–10].**

As I look at the world today, I have come to the conclusion that our hope is no longer in statesmen or politicians; our hope is no longer in science or education—they are all more or less failures. We are going to have to do what David did and what Israel will do in the future— start looking up. God is our only hope today.

PSALMS 65 AND 66

THEME: Songs of the Millennium

"To the chief Musician, A Psalm and Song of David." It is known as a restoration psalm—". . . of restitution of all things, which God hath spoken by the mouth of all his holy prophets since the world began" (Acts 3:21). The "restitution of all things" does not mean that everyone is going to be saved. Those who hold the doctrine of restitutionalism use this verse to support their theory. Exactly what are the "all things" which are to be the subject of restitution? In Philippians 3:8 when Paul said, ". . . I count all things but loss . . ." did he mean all things in God's universe? Obviously not. So here, the "all things" are limited by what follows. "The times of restitution of all things, which God hath spoken by the mouth of all his holy prophets since the world began." The prophets had spoken of the restoration of Israel. Nowhere is there a prophecy of the conversion and restoration of the wicked dead.

> **Praise waiteth for thee, O God, in Sion: and unto thee shall the vow be performed [Ps. 65:1].**

Sion is the same as Zion, and this verse is not speaking about a heavenly Zion. It is a geographical spot down here on earth. I have been to that place. I saw the sign that pointed the way to Mount Zion, and I went up there. And I didn't go to heaven that day, I assure you of that. It is a long hard pull up that elevation. When David speaks of Sion, he means that place.

> **Blessed is the man whom thou choosest, and causest to approach unto thee, that he may dwell in thy courts: we shall be satisfied with the goodness of thy house, even of thy holy temple [Ps. 65:4].**

As a redeemed people, they express their happiness.

> Thou visitest the earth, and waterest it: thou greatly
> enrichest it with the river of God, which is full of water:
> thou preparest them corn, when thou hast so provided
> for it.
>
> Thou waterest the ridges thereof abundantly: thou set-
> tlest the furrows thereof: thou makest it soft with
> showers: thou blessest the springing thereof.
>
> Thou crownest the year with thy goodness; and thy
> paths drop fatness.
>
> They drop upon the pastures of the wilderness: and the
> little hills rejoice on every side.
>
> The pastures are clothed with flocks; the valleys also
> are covered over with corn; they shout for joy, they also
> sing [Ps. 65:9-13].

Everything sings! This is a beautiful picture of the Millennium, when the desert blossoms like the rose and the earth at last is at peace.

Psalm 66 is "To the chief Musician, A Song or Psalm." Did David write it? We are not told, but he could have. We are not given any historical background for it at all, but many have guessed at what prompted its writing. It is a psalm of praise unto God and a wonderful psalm of worship.

> O bless our God, ye people, and make the voice of his
> praise to be heard [Ps. 66:8].

This verse looks forward to that day in the future when Israel will be restored to the land. Ezekiel tells us that in that day they will offer sacrifices. What is the explanation of it? Just as they offered sacrifices in the Old Testament that pictured the *coming* of Christ, in the future they will offer sacrifices that will look *back* to Christ's coming. Every lamb will point to ". . . the Lamb of God which taketh away the sin of the world" (John 1:29).

PSALM 67

THEME: Blessing and praise for the Millennium

This is one of the shortest prophetic psalms. It has only seven stanzas. Now I believe that numbers in Scripture have a meaning, but I also think you can go to seed in that direction. Seven seems to be not so much the number of perfection as the number of completeness; and, in a sense, when something is complete, perfection is always implied.

This psalm reveals the ultimate and final desire and purpose of God for this earth. It is a great psalm of the kingdom. It has been labeled by some (*The Expositor's Bible,* for example) as a missionary psalm. They give as its theme the outmoded, postmillennial interpretation of the church converting the world. Well, this is not a missionary psalm as such. Actually, the church is not in view at all. I do not believe we see the church in the Psalms except as a figure of speech or in a symbol. For example, we noted in Psalm 45 the church as ". . . the queen in gold of Ophir." This is a picture of the church with the Lord Jesus when He reigns on earth. Psalm 67 is a *prophetic* psalm. It looks beyond this age to the kingdom age. During the millennial kingdom you will see a converted world, a renovated world, a world in which God shall bless us, and all the ends of the earth shall fear Him. The curse will be removed and we will be able to sing songs of praise—even I will be able to sing the Hallelujah Chorus.

Now there is a difference between interpretation and application of Scripture. I am afraid that in wanting to be esoteric and intellectual, many theologians and Bible teachers have forgotten one of the simplest rules for the understanding of Scripture. And the simple rule is this: All Scripture is *for* us, but not all Scripture is *to* us. This psalm is *for* us, and not *to* us; and it gives us the perspective of missions. Now someone is going to say, "How can you possibly get missions into a psalm that looks beyond the church?" A great principle of hermeneutics (the science of interpretation) points out the difference between interpretation and application. *Interpretation* is definitive; it is like a mold—it is basic. That is, Scripture means *one* thing. It does not mean everything under the sun that you want it to mean. But there can also be an *application*, and the application may be elastic, although it must rest upon the interpretation if it is going to be accurate.

I can illustrate this in a simple way. A diamond, to be of practical value, must be cut, mounted in a proper setting, and worn on any finger it fits. Several years ago I was in Washington, D.C., for the first time. I went to the Smithsonian Institution, and among other things I saw the Hope diamond. I made an interesting observation. Many people were passing by the space exhibit, but everyone stopped to look at the Hope diamond. I suppose that reveals the covetousness in the hearts of all men. However, that diamond could not be worn on any finger, so it's of no practical value. If our country were invaded or some other terrible thing were to happen, I am told that the case in which the diamond rests would sink into a vault somewhere in the basement of that institution. As far as I can see, it is not doing anyone any good. It is of no personal worth at all. It is just a big diamond, ill-starred and ill-fated. To be useful it must be put in a setting. Scripture likewise must be put in a proper setting, which is interpretation. Then it must be placed on the finger of experience, and that is application. There is an old bromide that says, "If the shoe fits you, put it on." If you come to one of these psalms and it speaks to your heart (and God can speak to you in all of them), then it has a message to apply to your life. For example, in the Book of Revelation the Lord Jesus spoke to seven churches in Asia. His message had a local interpretation and a local application. He concluded His message by saying, "Hear!" That word is for the fellow who has ears. If you have ears, He is also talking to you. "He that hath an ear, let him hear what the Spirit saith unto the churches" (Rev. 3:13). There is an application for us in every one of the seven messages to the churches.

Psalm 67 is not a missionary psalm, I repeat, but it does contain some great principles that relate to God's missionary program for you and me.

Let us now summarize several interesting aspects of this psalm. "Bless us" is used three times. "Praise thee" is repeated four times.

There are three persons or groups mentioned: (1) God is referred to fifteen times, and the Trinity is there. (2) The nation of Israel, which is the "us," is mentioned six times. (3) The "nations" are mentioned nine times—and that means foreigners, different peoples and races, different strata of society, and you and me.

Notice how this psalm begins.

God be merciful unto us, and bless us; and cause his face to shine upon us; Selah [Ps. 67:1].

This verse is a reference to the Trinity. It is a reference to the great threefold Trinitarian blessing that God gave the nation of Israel when He prepared them for the wilderness march. That blessing is found in Numbers 6:24–26, which says: "The LORD bless thee, and keep thee [refers to the Father]: The LORD make his face shine upon thee, and be gracious unto thee [refers to Jesus]: The LORD lift up his countenance upon thee, and give thee peace [the work of the Holy Spirit]."

As we have noted before, some of the teachers of Israel refer to the "face of God" as the Messiah; and this is the Messiah, that is Jesus, the Christ, God the Son, our Savior. So here we have the threefold blessing of God the Father, God the Son, and God the Holy Spirit. The conclusion to this blessing is found in Numbers 6:27, which says, "And they shall put my name upon the children of Israel; and I will bless them." This Aaronic blessing will be fulfilled in the Millennium.

That thy way may be known upon earth, thy saving health among all nations [Ps. 67:2].

There will be no blessing for the earth until Israel is actually back in the land; and I do not mean as they are today, but in that day when the Lord puts them in the land. When that happens, Israel will be able to do what Isaiah speaks about in Isaiah 49:13, "Sing, O heavens; and be joyful, O earth; and break forth into singing, O mountains: for the LORD hath comforted his people, and will have mercy upon his afflicted." Verses 14–16 go on to say, "But Zion said, The LORD hath forsaken me, and my Lord hath forgotten me. Can a woman forget her sucking child, that she should not have compassion on the son of her womb? yea, they may forget, yet will I not forget thee. Behold, I have graven thee upon the palms of my hands; thy walls are continually before me." That is what God says concerning His people Israel. Either God meant what He said, or He did not; and, as far as I'm concerned, He meant it.

Let the people praise thee, O God; let all the people praise thee.

O let the nations be glad and sing for joy: for thou shalt judge the people righteously, and govern the nations upon earth. Selah [Ps. 67:3–4].

This is the marvelous promise God gave to Abraham: I will make you a blessing unto all peoples (Gen. 12:1–3). At His first coming the Lord Jesus made it very clear that salvation was of the Jews. At the Lord's second coming the earth will be converted. The greatest time of salvation, I believe, will be in the future. It is not possible for this passage to come true during this age; not until the Millennium will it come to pass. For Isaiah says, "And I will set a sign among them, and I will send those that escape of them unto the nations, to Tarshish, Pul, and Lud, that draw the bow, to Tubal, and Javan, to the isles afar off, that have not heard my fame, neither have seen my glory; and they shall declare my glory among the Gentiles" (Isa. 66:19). The day is coming when the world will be converted.

Let the people praise thee, O God; let all the people praise thee [Ps. 67:5].

What is the goal of God? Is it that we should get Israel back to the land? It would indeed be foolish just to be interested in getting them back into the land; but it would be no more foolish than to try to convert the whole world, for the church will not bring in the kingdom by preaching, I can assure you of that. Romans 11:25 makes it very clear: "For I would not, brethren, that ye should be ignorant of this mystery, lest ye should be wise in your own conceits; that blindness in part is happened to Israel, until the fulness of the Gentiles be come in." For how long? ". . . Until the fulness of the Gentiles be come in."

> **Then shall the earth yield her increase; and God, even our own God, shall bless us [Ps. 67:6].**

The curse of sin will be removed from the earth, you see.

> **God shall bless us; and all the ends of the earth shall fear him [Ps. 67:7].**

I want to make a comment that I believe is important. Suppose I should ask you, "What is the primary objective and purpose of missions?" What would your answer be? Someone might say, "The purpose of missions is to save souls." My response to that is that to save souls is not the purpose of missions. It is true that missions should result in the saving of souls, but that is not the primary purpose. Someone else might say, "We should preach the gospel to every creature in order that we might obey the command of our Lord Jesus Christ. Those are our orders. We are to preach the gospel everywhere. We are to get the Word of God out to people around the globe." While this is true, it is not the primary motive of missions. It is close but, honestly, I don't think that is quite it. Let me again quote verses 5 and 7 together: "Let the people praise thee, O God; let all the people praise thee. . . . God shall bless us; and all the ends of the earth shall fear him" (that means reverential trust in God). What is the final goal of missions? "Let all the people praise thee." The chief end of missions is to *glorify God.* That is the engine that is to pull the train of every mission program and of every Christian enterprise. The engine is to glorify God, and that which follows it is this: preach the gospel, get the Word out so people can be saved. The whole purpose is to glorify God. I wonder if we have lost that objective today? It is in the catechism I had to learn: Question: "What is the chief end of man?" Answer: "The chief end of man is to glorify God and to enjoy Him

forever." That is the purpose of man on earth. Why do you and I exist?
Are we here only "to eat the meat and fish and leave behind an empty
dish"? Is that all man is supposed to do? No, man is to glorify God.
We glorify Him when we get His Word out. We glorify Him when we
preach the gospel. We glorify Him when people are saved. But the
purpose is to glorify God.

PSALM 68

THEME: Song of deliverance that ushers in the kingdom

Here is a psalm of deliverance and victory. Whereas we saw the kingdom in Psalm 67, here we see the King in His glory and strength.

> **Let God arise, let his enemies be scattered: let them also that hate him flee before him [Ps. 68:1].**

This is a reference to Numbers 10:35. Each day when Israel was ready to begin the wilderness march, Moses would say, ". . . Rise up, LORD, and let thine enemies be scattered; and let them that hate thee flee before thee." What a wonderful way to begin the day's march!

The preceding psalm was a singing psalm, and this is another singing psalm—a song of triumph and glory!

> **Sing unto God, sing praises to his name: extol him that rideth upon the heavens by his name JAH, and rejoice before him [Ps. 68:4].**

"Sing unto God, sing praises to his name"—here, again, we see that man is to glorify Him, and God is moving toward that day when the earth will glorify Him. Men don't glorify God today; they take His name in vain.

> **Though ye have lien among the pots, yet shall ye be as the wings of a dove covered with silver, and her feathers with yellow gold [Ps. 68:13].**

The word *pots* should probably be changed to "sheepfolds." Deborah used that same Hebrew word in her prophetic song: "Why abodest thou among the sheepfolds, to hear the bleatings of the flocks? . . ." (Jud. 5:16). You will see that this was addressed to Reuben, because Reuben did not go out to battle. Evidently in both passages the word is used to describe an indifferent, an inactive, and a selfish condition. In this psalm it seems to have the same meaning—Israel was undecided and inactive. "Yet shall ye be as the wings of a dove"—the dove was a sacrificial bird and is a type of Christ. What a picture this gives us. Though they be negligent, though they are not moved by enthusiasm, yet the sacrifice of Christ will cover them.

This psalm could actually be called the psalm of the Ascension since we have a verse that is quoted in Ephesians 4:8: ". . . When he ascended up on high, he led captivity captive, and gave gifts unto men."

Thou hast ascended on high, thou hast led captivity captive: thou hast received gifts for men; yea, for the rebellious also, that the Lord God might dwell among them [Ps. 68:18].

When the Lord Jesus Christ ascended to heaven after His death, I think He did two things. First, He took with Him to heaven all those saints of the past who were in paradise. God had saved them on credit up to that time, but our Lord paid the redemptive price for them when He died on the cross. He took them (the spirits of just men made perfect) into the presence of God. Secondly, He gave gifts to men on earth so that today He carries on His work through those to whom He has given those gifts. Every person who is in the body of Christ has a gift—not all have the same gift, of course. As you can see, this is a marvelous verse.

But God shall wound the head of his enemies, and the hairy scalp of such an one as goeth on still in his trespasses.

The Lord said, I will bring again from Bashan, I will bring my people again from the depths of the sea [Ps. 68:21–22].

These verses speak of a glorious victory for the future. The one referred to as the "hairy scalp" is the Antichrist. In spite of what the
Antichrist will try to do, he will fail. God will bring His people from
even the depths of the sea. This is Israel's restoration.

**There is little Benjamin with their ruler, the princes of
Judah and their council, the princes of Zebulun, and the
princes of Naphtali [Ps. 68:27].**

These verses are talking about the children of Israel. There are those
today who believe that Great Britain is the ten lost tribes of Israel.
Perhaps they think little Benjamin really refers to Big Ben in London.
May I say to you that there are interpretations that are as wild as that
today. Little Benjamin simply means the tribe of Benjamin. It does not
mean anything else. But notice that little Benjamin has a great God.

**O God, thou art terrible out of thy holy places: the God
of Israel is he that giveth strength and power unto his
people. Blessed be God [Ps. 68:35].**

We also are little but have the same great God, and He gives us the
strength and power we need. Blessed be God!

PSALM 69

THEME: The silent years in the life of Christ

This is a great messianic psalm. It is another psalm of David, and it is unique because it deals with the silent years in the life of the Lord Jesus. It is also called a shoshannim, or lily, psalm because He is the Lily of the Valley as well as the Rose of Sharon, and He is altogether lovely. Next to Psalm 22 it is the most quoted psalm in the New Testament. Psalm 22 deals with the death of Christ; Psalm 69 deals with the life of Christ. I was drawn to this psalm when I was a student in college, and from that day to this it has been a favorite of mine. Psalm 22 is number one on the Hit Parade of the New Testament as far as quotes go, and Psalm 69 is second on the Hit Parade. It is quoted in the Gospel of John, in Romans, in Matthew, Mark, Luke, and Acts. Very candidly, I think there are many references to it which are not actual quotations. It is classified as an imprecatory psalm because verses 22–28 are what is known as an imprecatory prayer. Yet from that section the New Testament writers often quoted.

This psalm tells us about the silent years of Christ's childhood and young manhood, of which the Gospels tell us practically nothing. Dr. Luke tells us about an incident in the life of our Lord when He was twelve years old, and then we learn nothing else about Him until He is about thirty years old. What about that period of time? This psalm fills in some of the details. We see some of Christ's dark days in Nazareth and His dark hours on the cross. His imprecatory prayer is actually a cry for justice. This is the psalm of His humiliation and rejection. We begin with him way up north at Nazareth. We hear the heart sob of a little boy, a teenager, a young man:

Save me, O God; for the waters are come in unto my soul [Ps. 69:1].

Notice how he suffered. His physical suffering on the cross was bad enough, but I think some of the things He suffered in His life on earth were almost unbearable. I am confident that multitudes of us would have ended our lives if we had gone through what He did during His lifetime.

> But none of the ransomed ever knew
> How deep were the waters crossed;
> Nor how dark was the night that the Lord
>   passed through
> Ere He found His sheep that was lost.
>   ("The Ninety and Nine"
>   —Elizabeth C. Clephane)

During our Lord's last three hours on the cross he became the Lamb of God that took away the sin of the world. It was then that He was made sin for us. Although He suffered all during His lifetime, as we shall see, there is no salutary or saving value in those sufferings as far as we are concerned. He took the place of humiliation, and He took it voluntarily. The limitation of Christ as a human being was a self-limitation. You and I would like to know more than we now know; we would like to expand our knowledge and our understanding. In contrast to this, when the Lord Jesus became a man, He contracted Himself, He humbled Himself. In this state He cries out:

I sink in deep mire, where there is no standing: I am come into deep waters, where the floods overflow me [Ps. 69:2].

These are the floods of suffering which started when the Lord was born in a stable, which was probably part of an inn. The stable was a better place to be born because no one could see what took place that night except the cows, the oxen, and the sheep. They were better than the leering crowd that filled the inn. But in the stable He began His life in suffering.

Now we go to Nazareth where He was brought up. We are told:

**I am weary of my crying: my throat is dried: mine eyes
fail while I wait for my God [Ps. 69:3].**

During those thirty years there were times when His eyes were red
with weeping. The next verse tells us why.

**They that hate me without a cause are more than the
hairs of mine head: they that would destroy me, being
mine enemies wrongfully, are mighty: then I restored
that which I took not away [Ps. 69:4].**

This verse is quoted in John 15:25, "But this cometh to pass, that the
word might be fulfilled that is written in their law, They hated me
without a cause." The Lord quoted this verse and applied it to Himself. The enemies of the Lord hated Him without a cause; that is, there
was no justification for their hatred. Romans 3:24 says, "Being justified *freely* by his grace through the redemption that is in Christ Jesus."
Being justified freely is the same as being justified without a cause;
the Lord did not find any merit in me. The Lord didn't say, "That
fellow McGee down there is such a nice fellow, I'll justify him." You
can be sure he didn't say that! Rather, He said, "He is a poor lost sinner." He justified me without a cause within me. Now this psalm tells
us that they hated Jesus without a cause—they hated Him without a
cause that I might be justified without a cause. What a wonderful
truth this is!

**O God, thou knowest my foolishness; and my sins are
not hid from thee [Ps. 69:5].**

How in the world can this verse apply to the Lord? You must remember that He came to earth as a human being. He was holy, harmless,
undefiled, and separate from sinners. But the last few hours on the
cross He became sin for us. That was the thing He was resisting in the
Garden of Gethsemane. He prayed, "Let this cup pass." What cup?
The cup of sin, which was *my* cup and *your* cup of iniquity. The sin

that was put upon Him was awful for Him—it comes naturally for us—but because He was holy, His suffering was terrible.

> **Let not them that wait on thee, O Lord GOD of hosts, be ashamed for my sake: let not those that seek thee be confounded for my sake, O God of Israel.**
>
> **Because for thy sake I have borne reproach; shame hath covered my face [Ps. 69:6–7].**

There are two reasons He is bearing this: (1) They hated Him because of who He was, the same way the sinner hates the righteous person today. (2) He came to take a lowly, humble place on earth.

> **I am become a stranger unto my brethren, and an alien unto my mother's children [Ps. 69:8].**

This verse tells me a lot I would not know otherwise. Mary had other children, which confirms the record in the Gospels. Perhaps one day her boys, Judas and Joses, said to her, "Mother, we heard somebody down the street talking, and they said that Jesus is not really our brother. They said that nobody knows who His father is." He became an alien unto His mother's children. Do you think it was a happy home in which he was raised? It may have been a very unhappy home.

Note how it reads: "An alien unto my *mother's* children"—not His father's children because Joseph was not His father. He was "an alien" because they were half-brothers and half sisters. You see, this verse teaches the virgin birth of Christ.

> **For the zeal of thine house hath eaten me up; and the reproaches of them that reproached thee are fallen upon me [Ps. 69:9].**

This is a verse which our Lord also quoted—in reference to the temple. In the temple the Lord found men who sold oxen, and sheep, and doves for offerings. He also found money changers there. He made a scourge of small cords and drove them all out. "And [he] said unto them that sold doves, Take these things hence; make not my Father's house an house of merchandise. And his disciples remembered that it was written, The zeal of thine house hath eaten me up" (John 2:16–17). My, these men were religious and as busy as termites; in fact, they were doing just about as much damage as termites would. Oh, they were busy, but they were far from God.

When I wept, and chastened my soul with fasting, that was to my reproach [Ps. 69:10].

When He would fast or weep, His brothers would ridicule Him for it. They would tell Him that He was just putting on an act.

I made sackcloth also my garment; and I became a proverb to them [Ps. 69:11].

Do you know what that proverb was? The word that circulated around was that He was illegitimate. You know what people would call Him today.

They that sit in the gate speak against me; and I was the song of the drunkards [Ps. 69:12].

Those who are "sitting in the gate" are the high officials of the town, the judges. You see, the best people in Nazareth also spoke against Him. Nazareth was a little town that would not accept the Lord Jesus because it would not believe the fact that He was the Son of God.

"I was the song of the drunkards"—the drunkards at the local bar made up dirty little ditties about Him and His mother. This was His life in Nazareth. It was not nice. Do you know why He endured all of this? He was raised in a town where He was called illegitimate in order that I might be a legitimate son of God. There is nobody in heaven who is going to point a finger at Vernon McGee and say that he is not God's son. Do you know why? Because the Son of God bore that for me on the cross; He paid the penalty for my sins. My friend, you have no notion what He endured for thirty years in order that you might have a clear title as a legitimate son of God.

> **But as for me, my prayer is unto thee, O Lord, in an acceptable time: O God, in the multitude of thy mercy hear me, in the truth of thy salvation [Ps. 69:13].**

This verse is quoted in 2 Corinthians 6:2 which tells us, "For he saith, I have heard thee in a time accepted, and in the day of salvation have I succoured thee: behold, now is the accepted time; behold, now is the day of salvation."

The Gospel records tell us that our Lord prayed, but this psalm tells us *what* He prayed:

> **Deliver me out of the mire, and let me not sink: let me be delivered from them that hate me, and out of the deep waters.**
>
> **Let not the waterflood overflow me, neither let the deep swallow me up, and let not the pit shut her mouth upon me.**
>
> **Hear me, O Lord; for thy lovingkindness is good: turn unto me according to the multitude of thy tender mercies.**
>
> **And hide not thy face from thy servant; for I am in trouble: hear me speedily.**
>
> **Draw nigh unto my soul, and redeem it: deliver me because of mine enemies.**
>
> **Thou hast known my reproach, and my shame, and my dishonour: mine adversaries are all before thee [Ps. 69:14–19].**

We see His distress but also His assurance of deliverance and victory. Neither the deep nor the pit could hold Him. He was saved out of them.

The next two verses tell of our Lord's dark hours on the cross:

> **Reproach hath broken my heart; and I am full of heaviness: and I looked for some to take pity, but there was none; and for comforters, but I found none.**
>
> **They gave me also gall for my meat; and in my thirst they gave me vinegar to drink [Ps. 69:20–21].**

This, now, is His imprecatory prayer:

> **Let their table become a snare before them: and that which should have been for their welfare, let it become a trap [Ps. 69:22].**

This is quoted by Paul in his Epistle to the Romans: "And David saith, Let their table be made a snare, and a trap, and a stumblingblock, and a recompence unto them: Let their eyes be darkened, that they may not see, and bow down their back alway" (Rom. 11:9–10). Now there are some folk who consider the imprecatory prayers unchristian. But since it is quoted in the New Testament in reference to those who have rejected Christ, I see nothing unchristian about it. I feel that the imprecatory prayers have been greatly misunderstood. When we put them back into the position where they belong, we see they are judgment being pronounced upon the lost.

> **Let their inhabitation be desolate; and let none dwell in their tents [Ps. 69:25].**

This is quoted by Peter in Acts 1:20 in reference to Judas Iscariot.

> **For they persecute him whom thou hast smitten; and they talk to the grief of those whom thou hast wounded.**

Add iniquity unto their iniquity: and let them not come into thy righteousness.

Let them be blotted out of the book of the living, and not be written with the righteous [Ps. 69:26–28].

"Let them be blotted out of the book of the living" raises a question. There has been a great deal of debate on Revelation 3:5 which says, "He that overcometh, the same shall be clothed in white raiment; and I will not blot out his name out of the book of life, but I will confess his name before my Father, and before his angels." Apparently there is the book of creation, and when we are born we are recorded in that book—"Thine eyes did see my substance, yet being unperfect; and in thy book all my members were written, which in continuance were fashioned, when as yet there was none of them" (Ps. 139:16). Also there is a book of life for those who are saved. And there is the book of works. It would seem that the blotting out has to do with the works of the person who is already saved. There is no suggestion of a name being blotted out of the book of salvation. There have been many other explanations for this passage. Another one is this: When you are born, you are put in God's book of the living. I take it that you are a candidate for salvation. When you are blotted out of that book, you have crossed over the line and are no longer a candidate for salvation. Now here in Psalm 69 the "book of the living" is obviously the book of creation; and "not be written with the righteous" means that they will not be written in the book of salvation.

This psalm ends with a glorious song of praise.

I will praise the name of God with a song, and will magnify him with thanksgiving [Ps. 69:30].

The first time the Lord came to earth He came in humiliation. He is coming back to earth in exaltation. Those on earth will be the redeemed ones—they are the only ones that will be on this earth. And the only ones who will be in heaven are the redeemed. Friend, there are just two kinds of people in the world today. There are lost people and saved people—redeemed sinners and unredeemed sinners. You can distinguish quite easily which group you are in.

Then there is a verse about God's poverty program.

> **For the LORD heareth the poor, and despiseth not his prisoners [Ps. 69:33].**

God is going to bring justice to this earth some day, but justice will not be realized until He returns.

> **Let the heaven and earth praise him, the seas, and every thing that moveth therein [Ps. 29:34].**

What a Hallelujah chorus this will be when everything that moves praises Him!

PSALM 70

This is a lovely little psalm of David. Its contents can also be found in the last five verses of Psalm 40. One of the critics has said, "It is a fragment accidentally inserted here." I will agree with the critic if he will take out the word *accidentally*. It is called a song of remembrance. Why repeat it here? Because my memory is not very good, and God knew it wouldn't be. I can imagine that God said, "By the time McGee gets to this point in the Book of Psalms he will have forgotten all about Psalm 40, so I'll repeat it." There are some things to remember here.

> Make haste, O God, to deliver me; make haste to help me, O Lord [Ps. 70:1].

This is a cry for immediate help. I like that.

> But I am poor and needy: make haste unto me, O God: thou art my help and my deliverer; O Lord, make no tarrying [Ps. 70:5].

I fall into that class of the poor and needy, and He wants me to know that He is my helper, my deliverer. My friend, God is *for* the poor and needy, and He is our helper in this day.

PSALM 71

THEME: A psalm for old age

This psalm is an elegy, and it is a psalm for old age. It is obvious that the psalmist, possibly it was David, was an old man when he wrote this.

> Deliver me, O my God, out of the hand of the wicked, out of the hand of the unrighteous and cruel man.
>
> For thou art my hope, O Lord God: thou art my trust from my youth [Ps. 71:4–5].

He prays and trusts.

> Cast me not off in the time of old age; forsake me not when my strength faileth [Ps. 71:9].

This is a good psalm for us senior citizens. I find that this psalm means a little bit more to me than it did twenty years ago.

> But I will hope continually, and will yet praise thee more and more.
>
> My mouth shall shew forth thy righteousness and thy salvation all the day; for I know not the numbers thereof.
>
> I will go in the strength of the Lord God: I will make mention of thy righteousness, even of thine only [Ps. 71:14–16].

Now notice another definite reference to old age:

> Now also when I am old and greyheaded, O God, forsake me not; until I have shewed thy strength unto this

**generation, and thy power to every one that is to come
[Ps. 71:18].**

Now, friend, if you are a senior citizen, let me say this to you: Don't go
into a corner and sit in a rocking chair. God hasn't forsaken you, and
right down to your dying days He has kept you on this earth for a
purpose. To be candid, I am praying, "Lord, don't let me sit down in a
rocking chair *permanently.*" I love to sit in a rocking chair. Many of
my friends across the country have a rocking chair in their homes
with my name on it. They always drag it out when I come to visit. I
enjoy a rocking chair—but I don't want to stay there all the time. I
want to be active for the Lord right down to the end of my life.

> **I will also praise thee with the psaltery, even thy truth,
> O my God: unto thee will I sing with the harp, O thou
> Holy One of Israel.**

> **My lips shall greatly rejoice when I sing unto thee; and
> my soul, which thou hast redeemed [Ps. 71:22–23].**

As we grow old, let's not talk about our aches and pains, let's rejoice
in the Lord and sing His praises.

> **My tongue also shall talk of thy righteousness all the
> day long: for they are confounded, for they are brought
> unto shame, that seek my hurt [Ps. 71:24].**

It is all right to reminisce if we are talking about God's goodness. The
psalmist says, "My tongue also shall talk of thy righteousness all the
day long."

This is a wonderful psalm for us old folk!

PSALM 72

THEME: The King and the kingdom are coming

This is called "A Psalm for Solomon." The critic claims that Solomon wrote it, but I don't believe it, because the concluding verse says this: "The prayers of David, the son of Jesse are ended." This is a psalm of David written for his son, Solomon.

This psalm concludes what we call the Exodus section of the Psalms. The Book of Exodus concludes with the glory of the Lord filling the tabernacle, and this is a prophetic psalm in which the Messiah Himself comes and establishes His glorious kingdom on earth. Notice that He is the God of *righteousness:*

> **Give the king thy judgments, O God, and thy righteousness unto the king's son.**
>
> **He shall judge thy people with righteousness, and thy poor with judgment.**
>
> **The mountains shall bring peace to the people, and the little hills, by righteousness [Ps. 72:1–3].**

Also verse 7:

> **In his days shall the righteous flourish; and abundance of peace so long as the moon endureth [Ps. 72:7].**

Righteousness is the plank in the platform that no political candidate has ever had—as far as I can tell. The Lord Jesus will reign in righteousness some day. This psalm describes His glorious kingdom.

> **His name shall endure for ever: his name shall be continued as long as the sun: and men shall be blessed in him: all nations shall call him blessed.**

Blessed be the LORD God, the God of Israel, who only
doeth wondrous things.

And blessed be his glorious name for ever: and let the
whole earth be filled with his glory; Amen, and Amen
[Ps. 72:17-19].

Apparently God gave to David this great vision of the kingdom and
the reign of Christ when the whole earth will be filled with His glory.
This is what David had prayed for; so he says—

The prayers of David the son of Jesse are ended [Ps.
72:20].

David says, "My prayers are all ended; I am through praying." What
David had prayed for will be realized. He had nothing more to pray
for!

LEVITICUS SECTION

Darkness and Dawn (Sanctuary in View)
Psalms 73—89

As I said in the beginning, we are dividing the Book of Psalms according to the Pentateuch. The first forty-one psalms we call the Genesis section. Psalms 42—72 are known as the Exodus section. Now we come to Psalm 73 which brings us to the beginning of the Leviticus section. It corresponds to the Book of Leviticus because in this section—even in Psalm 73—the sanctuary is prominent. You see, the Book of Leviticus is the book of worship for the tabernacle and later for the temple. It is one of the greatest books in the Bible. Now as we come to this Leviticus section of the Book of Psalms, we find the emphasis upon the sanctuary and, in particular, on two aspects of the house of God. The Book of Leviticus emphasizes two things: that God is holy and that without shedding of blood there is no remission of sins—the key words are *holiness* and *sacrifice*. These two words will also figure largely in this Leviticus section of the Book of Psalms.

PSALM 73

THEME: *Perplexity about prosperity*

In this section are very wonderful psalms, and we begin with psalms of Asaph. Like David, this man was a musician. The first series of eleven psalms (73—83) was written by Asaph.

> **Truly God is good to Israel, even to such as are of a clean heart [Ps. 73:1].**

Immediately our attention is drawn to the fact that "God is good to Israel." Does that mean that He is good to every Israelite? No! His goodness is limited to those who are of a clean heart. Who would they be? Those who have come with their sacrifices, those who have a desire to serve God and walk with Him. My friend, if you are saved, you want to walk with God and fellowship with him. You want to have a clean heart. That follows just as day follows night. You cannot come to Christ and accept Him as your Savior, and continue to live as you did before. If you do, I cannot believe that you were saved in the first place. That is the explanation, and I feel that we need to hold to that rather tenaciously in our day. We are in the presence of God on the basis that He has cleaned us up. When we receive Christ, we have forgiveness of sins; we are washed—it is a washing of water by the Word of God. We are not only washed by the blood of Christ, but we are washed by the Word of God. The Word of God sanctifies us, and then we want to walk well-pleasing to Him.

Now this man Asaph who came into God's presence and could say, "God is good to Israel," had a problem. I think his problem may be your problem also—it certainly has been mine. The problem is this: "Why does God permit the prosperity of the wicked? Why is it that God's people seem to suffer more?" Many times, as a pastor, I found myself puzzled. I saw God's people tried. I saw God's people suffer. I saw the prosperity of the wicked, and it was hard for me to understand it.

It was brought home to me when our first child was born. In the hospital God took that child. I only heard the cry of that little one. All she ever did in her life was cry. I shall never forget the day she died. Across the hall from where my wife was, there was a very wealthy couple who had a baby boy, and their rich friends came to celebrate with them. As I drove into the parking lot in my old beat-up Chevrolet, they all drove up in Cadillacs. They went into the hospital with their champagne and celebrated the birth of the little boy. He was a precious looking little baby—all they desired, I guess. I shall never forget that night. It was summertime, and I went out on a balcony that was there and cried out to God. To be honest with you, I don't know to this good day why God took our baby and left the baby across the hall. They have money, and, boy, they live it up! I have seen write-ups about them, and they have been in trouble several times. Their little boy is now an adult, as my daughter would be. After all these years, I still don't have the answer. You may be thinking, *You are a minister, and you don't have the answer?* No, I don't have the answer. *Then how can you comfort others?* Well, I'll tell you how. Although I don't have the answer, I know the One who does, and He has told me to walk with Him by faith. He tests me by putting me in the dark. Then I'll reach out my hand and take His. In His Word He tells me that I can trust Him. Someday He will explain the whys of life to me.

Asaph had a problem like that. Asaph has already said that God is good to Israel—that believing remnant of which he was a part—but this question really bothered him.

> **But as for me, my feet were almost gone; my steps had well nigh slipped.**
>
> **For I was envious at the foolish, when I saw the prosperity of the wicked [Ps. 73:2–3].**

Asaph said, "I looked around me at my nation, and I noticed that the wicked among my people were the ones prospering, and the godly were not."

> **For there are no bands in their death: but their strength is firm [Ps. 73:4].**

"There are no bands in their death"—there are no pangs or pains in their death.

> **They are not in trouble as other men; neither are they plagued like other men.**
>
> **Therefore pride compasseth them about as a chain; violence covereth them as a garment [Ps. 73:5–6].**

I think again of the wealthy couple with the little boy baby; oh, how arrogant they were and filled with pride!

> **Their eyes stand out with fatness: they have more than
> heart could wish [Ps. 73:7].**

These folk have everything. As I think of it, I don't think they have
had the fun that I have had in this life, because when I got a new
something or other, it sure was a joy to me. It wasn't a joy to them
because they had it all along. "Their eyes stand out with fatness"—I
hadn't thought of that until I studied this psalm. They had puffs under
their eyes—they had been drinking too much and had too much night
life. The mother of that little fellow would have been beautiful if her
face had not shown so much sign of dissipation.

> **They are corrupt, and speak wickedly concerning op-
> pression: they speak loftily [Ps. 73:8].**

They don't mind walking on the poor. They insist that our children
have to go to integrated schools, but their children do not. Everyone
else must obey the law, but they somehow are exempt. As you look
around you, this is something that can make you bitter.

> **They set their mouth against the heavens, and their
> tongue walketh through the earth [Ps. 73:9].**

My, listen to these rich people on television today. They are the ones
who make the news. "Their tongue walketh through the earth," and I
know of nothing that enables it to walk better than television.

> **Therefore his people return hither: and waters of a full
> cup are wrung out to them [Ps. 73:10].**

God's people are taxed to death. We are told that some rich folk pay no
taxes at all. My, they really have it made!

> **And they say, How doth God know? and is there knowl-
> edge in the most High? [Ps. 73:11].**

They are not interested in God, and they don't think He knows anything about them.

> **Behold, these are the ungodly, who prosper in the world; they increase in riches [Ps. 73:12].**

Does that ever bother you? It bothers me.

> **Verily I have cleansed my heart in vain, and washed my hands in innocency [Ps. 73:13].**

Asaph says, "I have attempted to live for God, and it looks like it does not pay."

> **For all the day long have I been plagued, and chastened every morning.**
>
> **If I say, I will speak thus; behold, I should offend against the generation of thy children.**
>
> **When I thought to know this, it was too painful for me [Ps. 73:14–16].**

This problem worried Asaph. It gave him sleepless nights. Why do the wicked prosper?

Now we come to the answer:

> **Until I went into the sanctuary of God; then understood I their end [Ps. 73:17].**

When Asaph went into the temple of God, he understood the "end" of the wicked. He gained insight into the end reserved for the wicked. This is the reason the Lord Jesus gave a parable about a rich man and a poor man to illustrate afterlife. It is recorded in Luke 16:19–31. It tells us that the day is going to come when God will judge the rich. That rich fellow ended up in a place of torment even though the liberal preacher pushed him right into heaven at the funeral. Nice things were said about him. They praised him for his gifts of charity, but his end was a place of torment. The poor man wasn't even given a decent burial—his body was thrown onto a dump heap. But God's pallbearers were waiting for him—they were angels—and they took him right into Abraham's bosom. You have to stay close to God today, friend, or you will become bitter and cynical as you see the injustice in the world. Asaph found his answer in the sanctuary. I don't know the answer to your question because I don't know the answer to mine, but I know Someone who does. He didn't say He would tell me right now. He said, "You trust Me. I've got the answer." Someday in His presence He is going to explain it all to us. Also I know that He is going to show me that what He did was *best*. I don't understand that either, but that is what He is going to do.

Until then—

Nevertheless I am continually with thee: thou hast holden me by my right hand [Ps. 73:23].

I told you that He will take your hand. He took mine when my little girl died. He said, "Walk with Me." That is the lesson I learned, and this is the lesson the psalmist learned.

Thou shalt guide me with thy counsel, and afterward receive me to glory [Ps. 73:24].

I am with Him today. My life verse is Philippians 1:6, "Being confident of this very thing, that he which hath begun a good work in you will perform it until the day of Jesus Christ." Don't tell me that He won't, because He will; and that is the message of this psalm. "Thou shalt guide me with thy counsel, and afterward receive me to glory." I can't ask for anything better than that. So, no matter what happens, whether I understand it or not, I will simply trust Him; and, if you don't mind, I will go on with Him.

PSALM 74

THEME: A cry for deliverance when the temple is defiled by the enemy

In this psalm the temple is before us again, and this time it is being profaned. It is a maschil psalm, not of David but of Asaph, who is a Levite and a musician in the tabernacle.

> **O God, why hast thou cast us off for ever? why doth thine anger smoke against the sheep of thy pasture? [Ps. 74:1].**

The psalmist asks, "Why have You done this to us?" Then he cries out:

> **Remember thy congregation, which thou hast purchased of old; the rod of thine inheritance, which thou hast redeemed; this mount Zion, wherein thou hast dwelt [Ps. 74:2].**

He gives us the geographic location. The psalmist obviously is talking about the land of Palestine and the nation Israel.

> **Lift up thy feet unto the perpetual desolations; even all that the enemy hath done wickedly in the sanctuary [Ps. 74:3].**

Notice that it is the "sanctuary" that the enemy had profaned.

> **Thine enemies roar in the midst of thy congregations; they set up their ensigns for signs [Ps. 74:4].**

What has happened? This is prophetic of that terrible invasion by the forces of Antiochus Epiphanes. (He was a Syrian, in the family of one of the four generals who divided up the empire of Alexander the Great after his death). In 175 B.C. he plundered Jerusalem, profaned the temple by pouring the broth of a sow all over the holy vessels, and placed an image of Jupiter in the holy place. This was called the abomination of desolation in Daniel 8. In A.D. 70 the destruction of Titus the Roman who profaned the temple and leveled it to the ground was also a fulfillment. However there will be further fulfillment of Asaph's prophecy after the temple is rebuilt. During the Tribulation the final abomination of desolation will be revealed which will profane the holy place. You will notice that in spite of all of this persecution and discouragement a godly remnant will say:

For God is my King of old, working salvation in the midst of the earth [Ps. 74:12].

Now hear their prayer:

Remember this, that the enemy hath reproached, O LORD, and that the foolish people have blasphemed thy name [Ps. 74:18].

In other words, Israel is saying to God, "The enemy has taken us, and many of the people of our nation have been foolish—they have not turned to You." But there is a faithful remnant.

O deliver not the soul of thy turtledove unto the multitude of the wicked: forget not the congregation of thy poor for ever [Ps. 74:19].

The psalmist cries out, "O God, save us in the midst of trouble." He looks forward to that day of God's deliverance. No matter how bad your trouble is, my friend, He will also deliver you. He has delivered His people out of much worse situations than we have been in, and He will do even greater things for them in the future.

Arise, O God, plead thine own cause: remember how the foolish man reproacheth thee daily [Ps. 74:22].

This is a call to God to move in victory; it is a prayer that recognizes God's ability to do it.

This psalm is a prayer of Asaph. It is a maschil psalm, instructing you and me that we can trust God in all our troubles.

PSALM 75

THEME: *A song of deliverance*

This psalm is "To the chief Musician, Altaschith, A Psalm or Song of Asaph." Psalm 74 was a prayer of Asaph. Psalm 75 is a song of deliverance, a song of triumph that will come; therefore, it is a psalm of faith.

> **Unto thee, O God, do we give thanks, unto thee do we give thanks: for that thy name is near thy wondrous works declare [Ps. 75:1].**

Ultimately, God is going to protect His name on earth. What a wonderful, glorious truth this is which is put before us in this psalm!

> **When I shall receive the congregation I will judge uprightly [Ps. 75:2].**

This verse should read, "For I will take hold of the set time; I will judge in uprightness." This means that when the Lord comes it will be at a set time. When our Lord walked on earth, He took the place of self-humiliation. It was as a man on earth, that He said, "But of the day and hour knoweth no man, no, not the angels of heaven, but my Father only" (Matt. 24:36). The Lord is coming at that appointed time. You cannot rush Him. He will come at the predetermined time. No man knows the date or the hour, although there are a few prophetic teachers across the country today who seem to have a private wire to heaven and seem to know when the Lord is going to return. But I don't—and, of course, they don't either. The important thing to note is that there is a set time when the Lord Jesus is going to return.

> **For promotion cometh neither from the east, nor from the west, nor from the south [Ps. 75:6].**

Where will help come from? Not from the east, west, or south. You will notice that no mention is made of the north, because that is the direction the enemy will come from. Only *God* will be able to deliver His people. Psalm 75 is a prayer of thanksgiving to God before the event even takes place! How wonderful these psalms are! I trust they are a blessing to your heart.

PSALM 76

THEME: Prophecy of the Messiah upon the throne

As we study these psalms, I trust that you have your Bible open before you, and that you will read the entire text. These psalms are not only the Word of God, but their arrangement is important. I am not going to insist that the arrangement is inspired, but you will miss a great deal of the message if you ignore the arrangement because they do tell a story. There is a message that develops in each series of psalms. You recall that Psalm 74 was a cry for help—"Arise, O God." Psalm 75 was a song of thanks for God's deliverance out of the clutches of the northern power. They couldn't get help from the east or west or south, and the north was where their trouble was coming from. Russia will come from the north to invade the land of Israel, which we believe will be during the Great Tribulation Period. Now Psalm 76 shows the Lord Jesus reigning in His kingdom as King-Priest, the true Melchisedek. Man on this earth is in subjection to Him.

In Judah is God known: his name is great in Israel.

In Salem also is his tabernacle, and his dwelling place in Zion [Ps. 76:1–2].

Reading from Dr. Gaebelein's translation, which I have used from time to time, these verses say, "In Judah God is known; in Israel His Name is great. In Salem is found His Tabernacle, and His dwelling place in Zion" (*The Book of Psalms*, p. 298). *Salem* is the ancient name for Jerusalem and means "the habitation of peace." Four geographical places are mentioned. None of these places have to do with California or any state in the union, or any other country. Judah, Israel, Salem (Jerusalem), and Zion are all in Israel in the Mideast. The fact that this psalm has a blessing for us lies in its application, not in its interpretation, and I believe that all Scripture is *for* us.

There brake he the arrows of the bow, the shield, and the sword, and the battle. Selah [Ps. 76:3].

This is the day the prophet spoke of when he said, ". . . they shall beat their swords into plowshares, and their spears into pruninghooks: nation shall not lift up sword against nation, neither shall they learn war any more" (Isa. 2:4). Until the Lord Jesus Christ reigns, you had better not apply that verse to the United Nations, because it doesn't fit. Isaiah is speaking about the peace that will come to this earth when Christ comes back. Until the sin of the human heart is either dealt with in redemption or judgment, there can never be peace on earth.

Thou art more glorious and excellent than the mountains of prey [Ps. 76:4].

Dr. Gaebelein translates this, "Thou art shining forth gloriously above the mountains of prey." The "mountains of prey" refer to Jerusalem. That city has been besieged twenty-seven times. It has certainly been a mountain of prey! The enemies have been there.

The Lord is going to judge the arrogant and the proud who have walked on earth and those who have come against the city of Jerusalem.

The stouthearted are spoiled, they have slept their sleep: and none of the men of might have found their hands [Ps. 76:5].

Or, as Dr. Gaebelein has it, "Spoiled were the stouthearted; they fell asleep in their sleep." "They fell asleep in their sleep." That is an interesting expression. How can you do that? It means that the stouthearted were no longer alert or aware. The apostle John writes that the whole world lies asleep in the arms of the wicked one (1 John 5:19). And the Devil doesn't want the world to wake up. He says to Vernon McGee, "Hush! Don't give out the Word so loud. You'll wake them up." But, friend, I'm trying to wake up the babies by telling them that judgment is coming and also that there is salvation in Christ.

You will also notice that ". . . none of the men of might have found their hands." Waking out of sleep, they were like the Midianites in the days of Gideon when they were awakened by the sound of trumpets and saw the lights. They knew they had been taken, ". . . and all the host ran, and cried, and fled" (Jud. 7:21).

> **At thy rebuke, O God of Jacob, both the chariot and horse are cast into a dead sleep [Ps. 76:6].**

When the Lord comes again, at His rebuke both the chariot and the horse will be brought down into a deep sleep. At that time the Lord will shine forth gloriously. Isaiah 60:1 speaks of that day, "Arise, shine; for thy light is come, and the glory of the LORD is risen upon thee." We sometimes sing a song with these words at Christmas. Actually, this verse has no fulfillment at Christmas, at the birth of Christ. It will be fulfilled when the Lord comes again to this earth. It will be a great day, but it is still in the future. Isaiah 4:5 tells us more about this day: "And the LORD will create upon every dwelling place of mount Zion and upon her assemblies, a cloud and smoke by day, and the shining of a flaming fire by night: for upon all the glory shall be a defence." The glory that will be there will be the person of Christ.

The day of vengeance of our God will come.

> **Thou, even thou, art to be feared: and who may stand in thy sight when once thou art angry?**
>
> **Thou didst cause judgment to be heard from heaven; the earth feared, and was still,**
>
> **When God arose to judgment, to save all the meek of the earth. Selah [Ps. 76:7-9].**

These verses can be translated, "Thou, Thou must be feared, and who can stand before Thee when Thou art angry? From heaven Thou didst thunder forth in judgment—the earth feared and became silent, when God arose to judge, to save all the meek of the earth." In Revelation

6:17 John says, "For the great day of his wrath is come; and who shall be able to stand?"

When the Lord comes again to earth, all things are going to be put under His feet.

> **Surely the wrath of man shall praise thee: the remainder of wrath shalt thou restrain [Ps. 76:10].**

"For the wrath of man praiseth Thee, Thou restrainest the remainder of wrath." God says that He lets man go only so far. However, during the Great Tribulation it seems that the Lord will remove all restraint and let man go to the limit. Today man is being restrained. The Restrainer is the Holy Spirit. Who else can restrain evil in the world today? God is going to make the wrath of man to praise Him.

> **Vow, and pay unto the LORD your God: let all that be round about him bring presents unto him that ought to be feared [Ps. 76:11].**

The satanic raging against God and against His anointed He will restrain. And, as Psalm 110:3 puts it, "Thy [His] people shall be willing in the day of thy [His] power." His people vow and *pay* their vows. The Gentile nations are in submission to Him. "The kings of Tarshish and of the isles shall bring presents: the kings of Sheba and Seba shall offer gifts. Yea, all kings shall fall down before him: all nations shall serve him" (Ps. 72:10–11).

What a day that will be! My, this is a great psalm.

PSALM 77

THEME: Perplexity about the mercy and goodness of God

This psalm is "To the chief Musician, to Jeduthun, A Psalm of Asaph." You will remember that Jeduthun was the chief musician. Asaph wrote this psalm for him either to play or to sing. It reveals a time of deep soul-searching because of the perplexity in the minds of the people in that day. Faith has its problems, but faith can find the solution. The answer again is in the sanctuary. History reveals that God does not forget.

> **I cried unto God with my voice, even unto God with my voice; and he gave ear unto me.**
>
> **In the day of my trouble I sought the Lord: my sore ran in the night, and ceased not: my soul refused to be comforted [Ps. 77:1–2].**

A good time to seek the Lord is in the day of trouble. I received a letter from a man who had lost his position. He would never listen to our program until he was out of a job and had nothing to do. It was then that he got right down to the nitty-gritty and trusted the Lord as his Savior. It is well to cry to the Lord in the time of trouble.

"And he gave ear unto me." God will hear you, my friend, when you are in trouble. You can go to Him. He is *real*. Sometimes I hear a soloist sing, "It's real; it's real; I know it's real. . . ." The way they sing it and the way they live makes me wonder if it actually is real with them. My friend, it is real—not because I say it, or because it is written here, but because you find it out by experience. He has already told us to taste of the Lord and see whether He is good or not. Try this thing out.

"My sore ran in the night, and ceased not"—I don't think he was speaking of a physical sore but an open sore of the soul.

Here is another wonderful thing he did:

> I call to remembrance my song in the night: I commune with mine own heart: and my spirit made diligent search [Ps. 77:6].

It is a wonderful thing to be able to sing in the night. I don't mean that you sing out loud and wake everybody up out of sleep. "I remember my song in the night." The night is the time when you wake up and worry. Problems loom large—everything in the dark looks bigger than it really is. That is the time to remember your song in the night.

Now he raises some perplexing questions:

> Will the Lord cast off for ever? and will he be favourable no more?
>
> Is his mercy clean gone for ever? doth his promise fail for evermore?
>
> Hath God forgotten to be gracious? hath he in anger shut up his tender mercies? Selah [Ps. 77:7–9].

I would say that a practical atheist said these things, but I have asked the same questions. Maybe you have too. Do you realize that there are many of us believers who practice atheism? We, and I include myself, act as if God does not exist, as if He does not hear our prayers, as though He has thrown us overboard. We live as though God is no longer favorable and has stopped expressing His grace. My friend, God is good! He wants to be gracious to you and to me. Regardless of what you have done, God wants to be good to you.

> Thy way, O God, is in the sanctuary: who is so great a God as our God? [Ps. 77:13].

You will remember that as we began this Leviticus section of the Book
of Psalms I pointed out that it is called such because it is anchored in
the sanctuary, the Holy of Holies. "Thy way, O God, is in the sanctuary" is a reminder to us who are believers to not forsake ". . . the as-
sembling of ourselves together, as the manner of some is . . ." (Heb.
10:25). We are enjoined today to meet with God's people. God does
not want you or me to go off in a corner and enjoy the Word of God by
ourselves. We are to share the Word with others so that we can grow
together. I don't believe in super-duper saints. God won't let you get
way ahead of your brothers and sisters. We are in the family of God
and will have to share the Word and the blessing with each other.
Therefore the way of God is in the *sanctuary*. If you are going to find
the answers to your questions, you will have to meet with God's people.

I received a letter the other day from a Christian mother. She wrote:
"God has given me and my husband five wonderful children to guide
for Him. All of the children are saved except for the baby, who is sev-
enteen months old. We are fortunate enough to be members of a Bible-
teaching church, where the pastor is led by God instead of man. He is
one of those precious men of God who has been rebuked and has had
his life threatened because of his boldness for God. Our cup runs over
with joy as we see God work in the hearts of people and change their
lives." It is good to hear of a church like this. We hear a great deal of
criticism of churches, but there are many Bible-believing churches
still at work today. If you attend a church where the Word of God is
preached and taught, you should fellowship there and grow with the
congregation. You will find the answer to many of your questions.
The way in which the Devil works is subtle. His attack today is not a
frontal one. He attacks the men who stand for the Word. This is something of which we should take note.

Now here is a scene that has to do with the sea.

> **The waters saw thee, O God, the waters saw thee; they
> were afraid: the depths also were troubled.**

> **The clouds poured out water: the skies sent out a sound:
> thine arrows also went abroad.**

The voice of thy thunder was in the heaven: the lightnings lightened the world: the earth trembled and shook.

Thy way is in the sea, and thy path in the great waters, and thy footsteps are not known [Ps. 77:16–19].

This passage refers specifically to God's leading the people of Israel across the Red Sea.

Thou leddest thy people like a flock by the hand of Moses and Aaron [Ps. 77:20].

My friend, this has an application for us. God is able to deliver His people today from the flood tide of atheism and lawlessness and immorality. What a great, loving Shepherd He is!

PSALM 78

THEME: The history of Israel from Moses to David

This psalm is a maschil of Asaph, a psalm of instruction, covering Israel's history from Egypt to the time of David. In it we see the failure of the people and the faithfulness of God. It is a wonderful psalm, and it calls upon God to hear and answer.

First, it is the call of God to His people. He asks His people to listen to Him.

> **Give ear, O my people, to my law: incline your ears to the words of my mouth [Ps. 78:1].**

This is a long psalm, and we can only hit the high points; but I urge you to read the entire psalm in your Bible. It will bless your heart.

> **The children of Ephraim, being armed, and carrying bows, turned back in the day of battle.**

> **They kept not the covenant of God, and refused to walk in his law [Ps. 78:9–10].**

This is a direct reference to when Ephraim did not go to battle, and God took note of it. In a larger sense, Ephraim is typical of the conduct of all Israel and of *all* of God's people. It was Israel then; it is the church today. And God's faithfulness is unchanged.

> **And they sinned yet more against him by provoking the most High in the wilderness.**

> **And they tempted God in their heart by asking meat for their lust.**

> **Yea, they spake against God; they said, Can God furnish a table in the wilderness? [Ps. 78:17–19].**

Let me translate this a little differently to bring out the meaning: "And they sinned yet more against him by provoking the Most High in the wilderness. And they tested God in their heart by asking food according to their desire. Yes, they spoke against God; they said, 'Can God furnish a table in the wilderness?'" This represents the type of unbelief that is seen among believers today. It is practical atheism on the part of God's people.

Now notice what God did:

Man did eat angels' food: he sent them meat to the full [Ps. 78:25].

"Angels' food" is better translated *food of the mighty*—"Man did eat the food of the mighty; He sent them food to the full." He gave them all that they needed, yet they were doubting God and criticizing God.

This psalm of instruction concludes with this allusion to David:

He chose David also his servant, and took him from the sheepfolds:

From following the ewes great with young he brought him to feed Jacob his people, and Israel his inheritance.

So he fed them according to the integrity of his heart; and guided them by the skilfulness of his hands [Ps. 78:70–72].

David is a type of Him who is David's Lord and David's Son. God was faithful to them, and He is faithful to us today, my friend.

PSALM 79

THEME: Future of Israel in the Great Tribulation

This psalm is a prayer—not for you and me to pray, but for God's people, the nation Israel, in the Great Tribulation, which is the terrible day of trouble that is coming to them.

This is another psalm of Asaph, a great musician, who was probably the writer and arranger of them. He was contemporary with David and probably served as his assistant.

O God, the heathen are come into thine inheritance; thy holy temple have they defiled; they have laid Jerusalem on heaps [Ps. 79:1].

Although this psalm was prophetic at the time it was written, it accurately pictures the siege of Nebuchadnezzar and the subsequent Babylonian captivity. Also the Maccabean period brought such a calamity. This prophecy's ultimate fulfillment will be during the Great Tribulation.

Prior to the Babylonian captivity, the false prophets were saying that God would never allow their destruction and captivity. However, the city that the false prophets had said could never be taken *was* taken, and the inhabitants were carried away into captivity. The temple they said could never be destroyed *was* destroyed. The city, of course, was Jerusalem, and the people were the children of Israel. This happened several times, and it caused these people to cry out to God. The temple, the sanctuary, is the very center of things. Remember that this section of the Psalms corresponds to the Book of Leviticus which has as its theme the worship centering about the tabernacle and later the temple.

The dead bodies of thy servants have they given to be meat unto the fowls of the heaven, the flesh of thy saints unto the beasts of the earth [Ps. 79:2].

This horrible carnage was difficult for the people of Israel to understand. Why was God permitting this to happen to them? The false prophets had been continually telling them that it could not happen to God's people. Although the prophet Jeremiah had been faithfully giving God's warning of judgment to come, he had been discredited and labeled as a traitor to his nation. The Israelites could not understand why God had not protected them. This is still a question in our day. I understand that a great many Jews have become atheists because of the terrible persecution and suffering of their people in Germany during Hitler's dictatorship. Of course it is difficult for them to understand it. Maybe they have the same questions the psalmist has. But have they been faithful to God? Are they back in proper relationship with Him? Have they accepted their Messiah? Are they turning to Him? The answer, of course, is no. God has judged His people in the past and is judging them in our day. I feel that great judgment has come upon the church and will increase in the future. Judgment has come upon the nations of the world, nations like our own.

Hear their cry:

How long, LORD? wilt thou be angry for ever? shall thy jealousy burn like fire? [Ps. 79:5].

The Jews cry out, "Aren't you going to let up on us, O Lord?" Then they cry to God for forgiveness:

O remember not against us former iniquities: let thy tender mercies speedily prevent us: for we are brought very low [Ps. 79:8].

They pray, "Don't remember our former iniquities." But how will He be able to rub them out and forget them? Only through the death of Christ. When Christ is rejected—whether it be by Jew or Gentile, rich or poor, bond or free, male or female, black or white, red or yellow—there is judgment. You have to meet Him in judgment or redemption; there are only two ways.

Now listen to the plaintive cry of these suffering people:

> Help us, O God of our salvation, for the glory of thy
> name: and deliver us, and purge away our sins, for thy
> name's sake [Ps. 79:9].

The children of Israel had been making the boast that God was among them and would deliver them. God had not delivered them, and they were being subjected to ridicule. The heathen were making fun of them.

Notice the note of thankfulness on which this psalm ends:

> So we thy people and sheep of thy pasture will give thee
> thanks for ever: we will shew forth thy praise to all gen-
> erations [Ps. 79:13].

In that coming kingdom their sorrows and their tears will be gone forever, and so there will be praise from generation to generation.

PSALM 80

THEME: Prayer to the Shepherd of Israel

In this series of psalms there is a continuation of thought, a prophetic development. The Septuagint version has the inscription: "the Assyrian," which has led some expositors to place this psalm in a later time. However, because it is definitely a psalm of Asaph, a contemporary of David, we know it was written during the time of the Davidic kingdom. The inscription is "To the chief Musician upon Shoshannim-Eduth," which means "lilies." We have seen before that a beautiful lilies' psalm mentions the Messiah, the Lord Jesus Christ. It is a plea to the Shepherd of Israel to lead them again.

Give ear, O Shepherd of Israel, thou that leadest Joseph like a flock; thou that dwellest between the cherubims, shine forth [Ps. 80:1].

The "Shepherd of Israel" is none other than the Lord Jesus Christ. We have had a simile of the sheep and the Shepherd before.

"Thou that leadest Joseph like a flock" refers to the wilderness journey of the tribes of Israel when they advanced toward the Promised Land to take possession of it. Jehovah, the Shepherd of Israel, was their leader. Joshua was their human leader, but he acted under the Captain of the Host of the Lord. The psalmist appeals to God who had met with these people in the Holy of Holies.

Before Ephraim and Benjamin and Manasseh stir up thy strength, and come and save us [Ps. 80:2].

Why would Ephraim, Benjamin, and Manasseh be mentioned? I think the answer can be found in Numbers 2:17–24. If you read this portion of Scripture, you will find that in placing the tribes around the tabernacle, these three tribes were immediately behind the ark in the order of the march. It was the ark that led the children of Israel through the wilderness. Just as God had led them once before, the cry comes to lead them again.

> **Turn us again, O God, and cause thy face to shine; and we shall be saved [Ps. 80:3].**

This same refrain is repeated three times in this psalm (vv. 3, 7, 19). It is sort of a chorus.

> **O LORD God of hosts, how long wilt thou be angry against the prayer of thy people? [Ps. 80:4].**

This is a brief elergy here. It is a lament, a sad part of the psalm, and includes verses 4–6. The psalmist feels God is angry because He does not answer the prayer of His people.

> **Thou feedest them with the bread of tears; and givest them tears to drink in great measure [Ps. 80:5].**

This is one of the most remarkable verses in the Word of God. God has given His people "tears to drink" and tears for their bread—all they had to eat was tears. These are the tears of suffering. No nation has suffered as the children of Israel have suffered—and survived. Most other nations, had they been treated like the Jews, would have been exterminated and would have disappeared from the face of the earth. Israel has been drinking tears down through the centuries. Why? Israel has rejected the Shepherd. When the Lord was here, He beheld the city of Jerusalem and wept over it. Luke 19:41–44 tells us what He said as He wept, "And when he was come near, he beheld the city, and wept over it, Saying, If thou hadst known, even thou, at least in this thy day, the things which belong unto thy peace! but now they are hid from thine eyes. For the days shall come upon thee, that thine enemies shall cast a trench about thee, and compass thee round, and keep thee in on every side, And shall lay thee even with the ground, and thy children within thee; and they shall not leave in thee one stone upon another; because thou knewest not the time of thy visitation." This is a tremendous passage of Scripture and gives the reason the Jews have had tears to drink. On His way to the cross Jesus turned to some of the women in the crowd who were weeping and said, ". . . Daughters of Jerusalem, weep not for me, but weep for yourselves, and for your children" (Luke 23:28).

Turn us again, O God of hosts, and cause thy face to shine; and we shall be saved [Ps. 80:7].

That "face to shine" is none other than the face of Israel's Messiah, the Lord Jesus Christ.

Now here is another remarkable verse:

Thou hast brought a vine out of Egypt: thou hast cast out the heathen, and planted it [Ps. 80:8].

God brought the nation of Israel out of bondage in Egypt. God cast the heathen nations out of the land of Palestine and planted Israel, His vine, there. Israel built a temple in which to worship God. Then they were told that their temple would be destroyed and they would be put out of the land. Why? For the same reason that God put the heathen nations out of the land—they turned their backs upon God. The responsibility of Israel was greater than that of the heathen nations, because God had granted to them a privilege that no other nation had, which was the *visible presence* of God.

Thou preparedst room before it, and didst cause it to take deep root, and it filled the land [Ps. 80:9].

This verse is speaking about Israel, the vine that God brought forth out of Egypt and planted in the Promised Land.

The hills were covered with the shadow of it, and the boughs thereof were like the goodly cedars.

She sent our her boughs unto the sea, and her branches unto the river [Ps. 80:10–11].

The question arises:

Why hast thou then broken down her hedges, so that all they which pass by the way do pluck her? [Ps. 80:12].

For years after God planted His vine He put a hedge about the land. The people lived in the land for a good six hundred years. God did not permit any of the great nations of that day to destroy them. Egypt came against Israel and had victories but did not destroy them. The same was true of Syria and the Hittite nation. But the day came when God removed the hedge and let the enemies of Israel come in. Why? Because Israel had rejected the Shepherd of Israel.

Let thy hand be upon the man of thy right hand, upon the son of man whom thou madest strong for thyself [Ps. 80:17].

At God's right hand is the place of power. Who is at "God's right hand"? It is Israel's Messiah. David wrote, "The LORD said unto my Lord, Sit thou at my right hand, until I make thine enemies thy footstool" (Ps. 110:1). The Lord Jesus applied this to Himself when His enemies challenged His messianic claim (Matt. 22:44).

Back in Genesis 35 is the account of Rachel when she gave birth to her second son along the roadside that leads into Bethlehem. Benjamin was the baby, but she didn't call him that. When she looked upon that little fellow to whom she had given birth, she called him Ben-oni, which means "son of my suffering." But when Jacob looked upon him—I think the baby had eyes like his lovely Rachel—he said, "No, we won't call him Ben-oni, we'll call him Benjamin, because he is the son of my right hand." Benjamin is a picture, a type of our Lord Jesus who came to earth the first time as the Son of suffering. But today He is at God's right hand. Of Him the Father said, "Sit thou at

my right hand, until I make thine enemies thy footstool." And someday He will be returning from that position to this earth.

> **So will not we go back from thee: quicken us, and we
> will call upon thy name [Ps. 80:18].**

A better translation would be: "So will not we go back from Thee,
revive us, and we will call upon Thy name."

Now here is the chorus for the third time:

> **Turn us again, O LORD God of hosts, cause thy face to
> shine, and we shall be saved [Ps.80:19].**

In other words, "Restore us, O LORD God of hosts, cause Thy face to
shine upon us." This is a wonderful, wonderful psalm!

PSALM 81

THEME: A song of deliverance

This psalm, like so many of the others, is linked to the one that preceded it. In other words, we have a continuous story. The prayer in the preceding psalm was not a prayer for Christians; it is for the time of Jacob's trouble at the end of the age. The great prayer for us today is, ". . . Even so, come, Lord Jesus" (Rev. 22:20). And in the meantime we're to ask Him to help us get out His Word.

It is a song of deliverance. It begins on a high note. It is a soprano solo. It is inscribed "To the chief Musician upon Gittith, A Psalm of Asaph."

> **Sing aloud unto God our strength: make a joyful noise unto the God of Jacob.**
>
> **Take a psalm, and bring hither the timbrel, the pleasant harp with the psaltery.**
>
> **Blow up the trumpet in the new moon, in the time appointed, on our solemn feast day.**
>
> **For this was a statute for Israel, and a law of the God of Jacob [Ps. 81:1-4].**

I think the key to this passage is in the blowing of the trumpet at the new moon. This is all very proper because the new moon appears before the Sun of Righteousness arises with healing in His wings. He is coming to deliver them. It is a beautiful picture of the Feast of Tabernacles. Israel had four feasts that came at the beginning of the year: the Passover, the Feast of Pentecost, the Feast of First Fruits, and then the Feast of Tabernacles. This psalm sounds like the Feast of Tabernacles, also called the Feast of Trumpets. "For this was a statute for Israel, and a law of the God of Jacob." It was a great day. And its fulfillment is still in the future.

Hear, O my people, and I will testify unto thee: O Israel, if thou wilt hearken unto me;

There shall no strange god be in thee; neither shalt thou worship any strange god [Ps. 81:8–9].

The Lord reminds them of the past.

I am the LORD thy God, which brought thee out of the land of Egypt: open thy mouth wide, and I will fill it [Ps. 81:10].

This is a promise to Israel, and we should leave it that way, but there is a spiritual lesson for us in this verse. God did not lead me out of Egypt; but He did save me out of sin, which is the "Egypt" of this world. Now God says, "Open wide your mouth, McGee, and I will fill it with spiritual blessings." And He has done just that. God has been good to me.

But my people would not hearken to my voice; and Israel would none of me [Ps. 81:11].

In other words, "Israel would have none of me." They still have not turned to God. There is not much difference between the Israel side and the Arab side as far as their relationship to God goes, and there is not much difference between that land and the United States. In fact, I think the United States is in the worst spiritual condition, yet we are telling the world how things ought to be done. Because of our own failure I believe our nation should be in sackcloth and ashes. As a people, as individuals, we need to turn to God.

PSALM 82

THEME: God judges the judges of His people

This is a psalm that has been misunderstood. A critic who denies the deity of Christ will turn to this psalm and ridicule it. This is another prophetic psalm that looks to the future for God's earthly people, Israel. We see in connection with this the glory of the Lord—and it is wonderful when these two are brought together. This gives us a prophetic description of the judgment which God will execute during the Tribulation period when He saves the faithful remnant.

He begins on that note:

> **God standeth in the congregation of the mighty; he judgeth among the gods [Ps. 82:1].**

"God standeth in the congregation of the mighty"—this hasn't happened yet, but He will stand there during the Millennium.

"He judgeth among the gods." Whom is He calling *gods?*

> **How long will ye judge unjustly, and accept the persons of the wicked? Selah [Ps. 82:2].**

It is important to understand this verse of Scripture. Notice who are "the gods." God is calling the judges "gods" because they stand in His place and walk in His shoes, if I may use that expression.

> **Defend the poor and fatherless: do justice to the afflicted and needy.**
>
> **Deliver the poor and needy: rid them out of the hand of the wicked [Ps. 82:3–4].**

When the Lord Jesus Christ comes as the Judge of this earth, He is going to defend the poor, the fatherless, the afflicted, and the needy.

One of the big arguments against capital punishment is that rich people never have to pay the penalty of their crimes, and poor people have to pay in full. The argument is that because of the inequality the penalty should be abolished. God is saying to the judges, "I want you to defend the poor and the fatherless." The current discussion of giving the poor an equal opportunity is not new; it is as old as the Book of Psalms. When the Lord Jesus, as Messiah, reigns on this earth, He will defend the poor and the fatherless, the afflicted and the needy. Today judges are standing in God's place, and they are to do the same thing.

Now here is an interesting verse:

They know not, neither will they understand; they walk on in darkness: all the foundations of the earth are out of course [Ps. 82:5].

Certainly the world today is being shaken and is in great turmoil, and one of the great problems has been the judges of the earth. It is very easy for a judge to be like Pilate, to wash his hands, and say, "I don't believe in that uncivilized method of punishing people by capital punishment." He thinks he can escape in that way. But when those who have broken the law come before him, he ought to remember that justice is blind. If a rich man has committed a crime that deserves capital punishment, it should be meted out just as it would be to a poor man who committed the same crime. Unfortunately, very few rich people have to pay for their crimes.

I have said, Ye are gods; and all of you are children of the most High [Ps. 82:6].

What does He mean, "Ye are gods"? The Lord Jesus Christ Himself quoted this verse when the Jews questioned His deity. They accused Him of blasphemy because He made Himself God. In John 10:33-37 we read, "The Jews answered him, saying, For a good work we stone thee not; but for blasphemy; and because that thou, being a man, makest thyself God. Jesus answered them, Is it not written in your law,

I said, Ye are gods? If he called them gods, unto whom the word of God came, and the scripture cannot be broken; Say ye of him, whom the Father hath sanctified, and sent into the world, Thou blasphemist; because I said, I am the Son of God? If I do not the works of my Father, believe me not."

Jesus was telling these Jews that they were sitting in judgment and, when one sits in the place of judgment, he is taking the place of God. Many saints are guilty of that type of thing. They sit in judgment on other saints. Paul says, "But with me it is a very small thing that I should be judged of you, or of man's judgment: yea, I judge not mine own self. For I know nothing by myself; yet am I not hereby justified: but he that judgeth me is the Lord. Therefore judge nothing before the time, until the Lord come, who both will bring to light the hidden things of darkness, and will make manifest the counsels of the hearts: and then shall every man have praise of God" (1 Cor. 4:3–5). Paul is saying that he is going to stand before God someday and because of that he doesn't even judge *himself*. My friend, when you start judging someone you are acting for God, and you are a god when you have taken that position of judging. I am fearful of our nation with so many godless people seeking office. They know nothing of the background of this country which was founded upon the Word of God; they are not in spiritual tune with the founding of this nation.

Years ago I was greatly impressed by that judge in New York City who presided at the trial of a husband and wife who were charged with being spies. The judge was a Jew, and he said that the night before he handed down his judgment was spent in prayer. I was impressed with that. Why? He was going to hand down a harsh judgment; he was going to stand in the place of God when he made the decision. That judge was actually standing in the place of God when he judged the lives of these two people who would have to pay for their crime against the government. A man in that position ought to be a godly man. He should be a man of prayer. The big problem in our contemporary society is not so much with the criminal as it is with the judges and the breakdown of law and order. It is strange that the breakdown of law and order has begun with the law profession and not really with the criminal element.

Any time that you pass judgment on a person, you stand in the position of God. Parents ought to recognize that. What does God say to a little fellow growing up in a home? He says, "Children, obey your parents in all things: for this is well pleasing unto the Lord" (Col. 3:20). But wait a minute—what if his parents don't tell him to do the right things and don't bring him up the way they should? There are many parents like that today. God says, "I am going to hold them responsible. They are in My place. They occupy that position because I have said to that little boy, 'My son, hear the instruction of thy father, and forsake not the law of thy mother'" (Prov. 1:8). God help the father or the mother who does not lead their child in a godly pathway. Someone has asked the question, "What is worse than going to hell?" The answer given by a great preacher in the South years ago was this: "To go to hell and recognize the voice of your son and ask, 'Son, what are you doing here?' and hear him answer, 'Dad, I followed you!'"

This is a tremendous psalm. God says to the judges, "Be sure you judge accurately. Ye are gods, and all of you are children of the Most High."

But ye shall die like men, and fall like one of the princes [Ps. 82:7].

God reminds the judges, who stand in the place of God, that they are still human beings, and the day is coming when they will have to stand before God and be judged.

Arise, O God, judge the earth: for thou shalt inherit all nations [Ps. 82:8].

This will be a prayer of the nation Israel. I feel that I could join in that prayer. "O God, judge this earth. O God, You are going to inherit all the nations. This earth is Yours. You judge it." I believe this is a prayer all of us can pray in this day in which we live.

PSALM 83

THEME: A cry for judgment

This is "A Song or Psalm of Asaph." This is the last psalm of the Asaph series and a rather puzzling one. The fact of the matter is that you cannot fit it into the history of the nation of Israel. Since you cannot, the idea is to guess at it, and there have been some wild guesses. This is an imprecatory prayer, a cry for justice. The psalmist prays for God to deliver His people from their enemies.

> **Keep not thou silence, O God: hold not thy peace, and be not still, O God.**

> **For, lo, thine enemies make a tumult: and they that hate thee have lifted up the head [Ps. 83:1-2].**

Whoever the enemy is here, he hates God. But isn't that always the case with the enemy?

> **They have taken crafty counsel against thy people, and consulted against thy hidden ones.**

> **They have said, Come, and let us cut them off from being a nation; that the name of Israel may be no more in remembrance [Ps. 83:3-4].**

This refers to those who have plotted the destruction of the nation Israel. There are those who have tried to fit this psalm into the time of Jehoshaphat, and others who have attempted to fit it into other historical periods. The important thing for us to note is that the enemies of God express their hatred toward Him.

Now we begin with the section of this psalm that is difficult to fit into history.

For they have consulted together with one consent: they are confederate against thee:

The tabernacles of Edom, and the Ishmaelites; of Moab, and the Hagarenes;

Gebal, and Ammon, and Amalek; the Philistines with the inhabitants of Tyre;

Assur also is joined with them: they have holpen the children of Lot. Selah [Ps. 83:5–8].

"Assur" is Assyria. "The children of Lot" would be Moab and Ammon. The names in this portion of God's Word are His enemies. There is no place in history where they seem to fit in; and that makes it a very remarkable section, because it appears that these verses look to the future. Apparently these nations which were in existence at one time will appear again in the future.

At the present time Israel is surrounded by Arab nations who are apparently joined together not so much as Arabs but as Moslems. They are opposed to the nation Israel. It looks as though the nations mentioned in these verses will come back into existence during the last days. They are not in existence now, and there is nothing to which they correspond. This fact makes Psalm 83 a very remarkable passage of Scripture.

The remainder of this psalm is an imprecatory prayer. It asks for God's judgment. It is retrospective in the sense that the psalmist is saying, "Judge as You have done it in the past."

Do unto them as unto the Midianites; as to Sisera, as to Jabin, at the brook of Kison:

Which perished at En-dor: they became as dung for the earth [Ps. 83:9–10].

In the Book of Judges we read how God judged those nations. There are those who say that God will not judge that way in the future. He

won't? He has judged that way in the past. God has not changed.
What He has done in the past, He will do in the future. For that reason
this is impressive.

Let me remind you that this is not the way we, as believers today,
should pray. We should pray for our enemies—not that God would
punish them, but that they might be converted, that they might turn to
God.

This is a prayer for Israel to pray:

> O my God, make them like a wheel; as the stubble be-
> fore the wind [Ps. 83:13].

Do you remember reading about the great big wheel that the oxen used
to pull around to beat out the grain and crush the stubble? The psalmist is saying, "Deal with our enemies that way, O Lord."

> As the fire burneth a wood, and as the flame setteth the
> mountains on fire [Ps. 83:14].

In other words, "Be like a forest fire!"

Now note the conclusion:

> That men may know that thou, whose name alone is JE-
> HOVAH, art the most high over all the earth [Ps. 83:18].

I am convinced that the only way this world is going to know that God
is God is for Him to move in judgment. The goodness of God ought to
lead men to repentance, but it doesn't. If men were at all sensitive to
the presence and person of God, it would lead them to His presence,
but it actually drives them farther away from God. We are an affluent
nation now. When we were a frontier nation, pioneering, fighting our
way across to the West, we depended on God, but today we think we
don't need Him. However, it looks to me as if we need Him desper-
ately.

PSALM 84

THEME: A deep desire for God's house

This is a psalm in which the Levitical emphasis is prominent. It is a psalm for the sons of Korah. The sons of Korah served in the tabernacle and later in the temple. Let's go back to 1 Chronicles 26 to see the background of this family. "Concerning the divisions of the porters: Of the Korhites was Meshelemiah the son of Kore, of the sons of Asaph" (1 Chron. 26:1). Then it gives a long list of that family of the Korhites. Now Korah, you may recall, led the rebellion against Moses, and he was judged for it. But now, by the grace of God, these descendants of his are serving in the tabernacle and in the temple of God. Then 1 Chronicles 26:12–13 says, "Among these were the divisions of the porters, even among the chief men, having wards one against another, to minister in the house of the LORD. And they cast lots, as well the small as the great, according to the house of their fathers, for every gate." A man was assigned to every gate. Lots were cast for the jobs. Strong, robust Levites guarded the tabernacle, and later they watched over every entrance to the temple. So the tabernacle and the temple are prominent in this psalm.

> **How amiable are thy tabernacles, O LORD of hosts!**
>
> **My soul longeth, yea, even fainteth for the courts of the LORD; my heart and my flesh crieth out for the living God [Ps. 84:1–2].**

Is this your heart cry today? Do you love to meet with God's people? I recognize that you don't get much fellowship in some churches today. In fact, you get more gossip and criticism than you get anything else. However, the place for fellowship is a church, and there are some *wonderful* churches throughout our land. I hope there is one in your neighborhood where the Word of God is preached and Christ is ex-

alted. If there is, that is where you should seek the fellowship of believers. That is where you will grow and be blessed.

Now this is lovely. These sons of Korah serving in the tabernacle
and later in the temple saw this:

> **Yea, the sparrow hath found an house, and the swallow
> a nest for herself, where she may lay her young, even
> thine altars, O LORD of hosts, my King, and my God [Ps.
> 84:3].**

I think the sparrows built nests around the temple. The man who
wrote this psalm, as he looked up and saw them, said, "I want to
dwell like that. I want to live that close to God." The Lord Jesus said to
consider the little sparrows. They are not worth anything. In fact, you
would like to get rid of them the way they chatter around and mess up
everything. They are dirty little birds. The Lord Jesus said, "Are not
two sparrows sold for a farthing? and one of them shall not fall on the
ground without your Father" (Matt. 10:29). Not one sparrow falls but
what the Father sees it. Actually, the language is stronger than that. He
says that the sparrow falls into the lap of your Father. He knows all
about it.

> **Behold, O God our shield, and look upon the face of
> thine anointed [Ps. 84:9].**

The psalmist can say, "Behold, O God our shield." God is our shield.
"And look upon the face of thine anointed." This is a reference to the
Messiah. Christ, the Messiah, revealed the face of God on earth.

The sanctuary, as we saw in the Book of Leviticus, was the very
center of the life of Israel. There was a day when the church was the
center of the social life in this country. It is not even the center of
religious life today, but it should be.

> **For a day in thy courts is better than a thousand. I had
> rather be a doorkeeper in the house of my God, than to
> dwell in the tents of wickedness [Ps. 84:10].**

He says, "A day in Thy courts is better than a thousand days anywhere else. I had rather be a doorkeeper in the house of my God, than to dwell in the tents of wickedness," and that's what the sons of Korah were—doorkeepers. He says, "I would rather have my job than to be a rich man living far from God." There are some folk who look at their watches on Sunday morning to see if the preacher is going overtime. The psalmist says, "I'd rather spend one day in God's house than a thousand anywhere else." What a glorious psalm this is, and what a rebuke it is to many of us.

PSALM 85

THEME: Future restoration of Israel

This psalm is "To the chief Musician, A Psalm for the sons of Korah." Certain critics have attempted to identify this psalm with the return of the people to the land under Ezra and Nehemiah. Actually it has no reference to that at all. The reason critics do this is because they do not recognize the fact that the Psalms are prophetic.

We are in a section where we have several writers of the Psalms and the amazing thing is that these psalms have been put together to tell a story. Although I do not insist upon the inspiration of the arrangement, it certainly looks as if God had the oversight of it. We have seen that they appear in series—a cluster here and a cluster there—that present a prophetic picture. This psalm looks to the future, and I have no confidence in any translation or interpretation made by a man who does not believe this is the very Word of God. I feel like a certain minister in Southern California who says, "We might as well trust a lunatic for a lawyer, a quack for a physician, a wolf for a sheepdog, or an alligator for a babysitter, as to trust a modernist's translation of the Word of God or proclamation of the Word of God." I say amen to that. My feeling is that we need expositors who believe the Bible is the Word of God and God knows the future as well as He knows the past.

Now note this prophetic picture:

> LORD, thou hast been favourable unto thy land: thou hast brought back the captivity of Jacob [Ps. 85:1].

Many critics assume that this verse refers to the return of the Jews to their land from the Babylonian captivity, but in reality only a small remnant returned to the land at that time. Less than sixty thousand people came back. The bulk of the people did not return. Rather than referring to the return after the Babylonian captivity, it looks forward to the kingdom age when God brings all of His people back into the land.

Thou hast forgiven the iniquity of thy people, thou hast covered all their sin. Selah [Ps. 85:2].

What a glorious picture this is! It can only refer to the future. It certainly did not depict the condition after the Babylonian captivity. If you think it does, read the Books of Ezra, Nehemiah, Haggai, Zechariah, and Malachi. Why, Malachi severely rebukes the people because their hearts are far from God. Oh, they were going to the temple and bringing sacrifices, but their hearts were far away from God. This psalm presents an entirely different picture.

Thou hast taken away all thy wrath: thou hast turned thyself from the fierceness of thine anger [Ps. 85:3].

This looks forward to the time when the judgments are over for Israel. The worst time for this nation and for the world is still in the future. The Great Tribulation is going to be global in its extent, and it will be a time of judgment. Satan will be turned loose, and the Holy Spirit will not be restraining evil. The lid will be taken off. The fellow who wants to paint the town red will have to have a brush that is big enough and plenty of paint to do it. God is going to let men go the limit, and then He is going to judge them.

For the child of God in this day, the judgment for sin is over. The sin question was settled when Jesus died on the cross for our sins. As the song writer put it, "The old account was settled long ago." But there is something that does trouble me: it is the fact that I will have to stand before the judgment seat of Christ, as will every believer, to give an account of my life and my works. Our works are going to be tried by fire. "Every man's work shall be made manifest: for the day shall declare it, because it shall be revealed by fire; and the fire shall try every man's work of what sort it is. If any man's work abide which he hath built thereupon, he shall receive a reward. If any man's work shall be burned, he shall suffer loss: but he himself shall be saved; yet so as by fire" (1 Cor. 3:13–15). I'm not sure about some of my works. No wonder that Paul didn't even judge himself because God alone can judge. I hope He will say, "Well done, thou good and faithful servant," but I'll have to wait and see.

During the Great Tribulation there is going to be brought together into a focal point everything in the way of judgment and evil, which is the reason I don't want to be here when it happens. And I don't think I will be here. To say that the church goes through that period is to miss entirely what is meant by the Great Tribulation.

> **Turn us, O God of our salvation, and cause thine anger toward us to cease.**
>
> **Wilt thou be angry with us for ever? wilt thou draw out thine anger to all generations? [Ps. 85:4–5].**

The day is coming when the suffering of these people will cease. As we saw in a previous psalm, their history has been one of tears to drink and tear-sandwiches to eat—that was their diet. The day is coming when it will be over. God will come and wipe away all of their tears.

> **Wilt thou not revive us again: that thy people may rejoice in thee? [Ps. 85:6].**

Today we need revival in our churches for several reasons. One reason is there is a lack of *joy* in the lives of believers. It should be there, but it is not.

> **Shew us thy mercy, O LORD, and grant us thy salvation [Ps. 85:7].**

This is something into which all of our hearts can enter. God hates evil and will judge it, but He is also a God of mercy and salvation to those who turn to Him.

> I will hear what God the LORD will speak: for he will
> speak peace unto his people, and to his saints: but let
> them not turn again to folly [Ps. 85:8].

When God's final judgment of sin takes place, His people will no longer turn to folly. They will not return to their sins because sin will be removed from the universe.

> Surely his salvation is nigh them that fear him; that
> glory may dwell in our land [Ps. 85:9].

There is no glory in Israel today. I love to visit that land, but I see nothing in the way of glory there, only a pile of rocks. Of course there are many places which are sacred to us as Christians.

Now this is one of the most remarkable verses in Scripture:

> Mercy and truth are met together; righteousness and
> peace have kissed each other [Ps. 85:10].

"Mercy and truth" haven't met each other in our day. "Righteousness and peace have kissed each other"—they aren't even on speaking terms today. One of the reasons we cannot have peace in this world is because we do not have righteousness in the world. Things have to be right, my friend, before there can be peace in the world. Things are not "right" today—they are not right in my neighborhood, or anywhere, and maybe things are not right in our lives. Until things are right, there will be no peace on earth. This is a great verse!

> Righteousness shall go before him; and shall set us in
> the way of his steps [Ps. 85:13].

When the Lord Jesus Christ reigns, He will reign in righteousness.

PSALM 86

THEME: David prays for the future kingdom

We have come now to another Davidic psalm, and it is a prayer of David.

It is remarkable in that it introduces another name for God. We have seen in former psalms that the names *Elohim*, which speaks of God as Creator, and *Jehovah*, which speaks of God as Savior, have been used. In this psalm another name for God appears seven times. It is *Adonai*, of which the English translation is "Lord." Adonai is the name of God which the pious Jew used (and still does) instead of Jehovah. When an orthodox Jew comes to the name Jehovah—the sacred tetragram YHWH—he doesn't pronounce it. In fact, the pronunciation has been lost, and today scholars debate about whether it should be pronounced Jehovah or Yahweh or something else. The orthodox Jew, considering the name Jehovah too sacred to voice, substitutes the name *Adonai*. Adonai refers to God as our Savior, the One who is the holy God, the One who has been able to extend mercy unto us.

Because Adonai occurs seven times in this psalm, it is considered a messianic psalm by some scholars. However, I do not think it could be called a messianic psalm in the strict sense of the word because of the nature of the prayer. For an example:

> **Teach me thy way, O Lord; I will walk in thy truth: unite my heart to fear thy name [Ps. 86:11].**

There is no way that you can apply this verse to the Lord Jesus. He would never need to pray a prayer like this, because He *came* to do the Father's will. But this verse can apply to you and me. We need to be taught God's way and His truth. Our hearts need to be united to fear His name. Christ came to do the will of His Father, and He did it. It is different with us. F. W. Grant has made a remarkable statement in this regard: "This is indeed what is everywhere the great lack among the people of God. How much of our lives is not spent in positive evil, but frittered away and lost in countless petty diversions which spoil effectually the positiveness of our testimony for God! How few can say with the Apostle [Paul], 'This one thing I do.' We are on the road—not at least, intentionally off it—but we stop to chase butterflies among the flowers, and make no serious progress. How Satan must wonder when he sees us turn away from 'the kingdoms of the world and the glory of them,' when realized as his temptation, and yet yield ourselves with scarce a thought to endless trifles, lighter than a thistledown for which the child spends all his strength, and we laugh at him. If we examined our lives carefully in such an interest as this, how we would realize the multitude of needless anxieties, or self-imagined duties, of permitted relaxations, of 'innocent trifles,' which incessantly divert us from that in which alone is profit. How few perhaps would care to face such an examination day by day of the unwritten history of their lives."

There are many Christian workers today who are not in open sin, but they sure are lazy. They kill time doing this and that, and they are busy here and there, but the main business remains undone. They are not guarding the stuff, and they are not alert in serving the Lord. How we need to pray, "Unite my heart to fear thy name."

The psalmist's prayer that preceded it is, "Teach me thy way, O LORD," which is, I think, the solution for a wandering, divided heart. The first thing that the apostle Paul said after he was converted was, ". . . Lord, what wilt thou have me to do? . . ." (Acts 9:6). The psalmist had the answer, "Teach me thy way, O LORD." And the Lord has promised to teach His children, "I will instruct thee and teach thee in the way which thou shalt go: I will guide thee with mine eye" (Ps. 32:8).

"I will walk in thy truth" should be our response, which means we should walk in the light that the Word of God gives us.

Then He will receive the praise of our whole heart. When our heart is united and devoted to Him, the greater our praise will be.

I will praise thee, O Lord my God, with all my heart: and I will glorify thy name for evermore [Ps. 86:12].

PSALM 87

THEME: Zion, the city of God

This psalm is "A Psalm or Song for the sons of Korah." Actually, I think it is a psalm by the sons of Korah. It is a song that deals with Zion, the city of God, and speaks of the glorious future of Jerusalem. The nations will come to Jerusalem to worship. I hear people today sing, "We're marching to Zion, that wonderful city of God." I am afraid that song is meaningless, because Zion is a geographical spot on this earth. When I was with a tour in Israel, several of us were in a car together riding toward Zion, which is the highest elevation in the city of Jerusalem. None of us could sing very well, but we sang as we rode along, "We're marching to Zion, that wonderful city of God." Actually we were riding, not marching, but at least we were headed for Zion.

His foundation is in the holy mountains [Ps. 87:1].

That is where the government of the world will one day be. Isaiah 2:2 tells us, "And it shall come to pass in the last days, that the mountain of the LORD's house shall be established in the top of the mountains, and shall be exalted above the hills; and all nations shall flow unto it." Zechariah 2:10–11 says, "Sing and rejoice, O daughter of Zion: for, lo, I come, and I will dwell in the midst of thee, saith the LORD. And many nations shall be joined to the LORD in that day, and shall be my people: and I will dwell in the midst of thee, and thou shalt know that the LORD of hosts hath sent me unto thee."

Remember that we are still in the section that is known as the Leviticus section, and the tabernacle and temple are the very heart of it.

The LORD loveth the gates of Zion more than all the dwellings of Jacob.

Glorious things are spoken of thee, O city of God. Selah [Ps. 87:2–3].

This same view was expressed before in Psalm 48, "Great is the Lord, and greatly to be praised in the city of our God, in the mountain of his holiness. Beautiful for situation, the joy of the whole earth, is mount Zion, on the sides of the north, the city of the great King" (Ps. 48:1-2).

I will make mention of Rahab and Babylon to them that know me: behold Philistia, and Tyre, with Ethiopia; this man was born there [Ps. 87:4].

"Rahab" is not the harlot of Jericho, but Egypt (see Isa. 51:9; Ps. 89:10). It represents the southern world power, and "Babylon" represents the northern. The name *Rahab* means "tumult" and *Babylon* means "confusion"—the tumult and confusion of these nations will end when Christ is reigning in Zion. It is very interesting to see that Zion will be the birthplace of many nations. When the Lord Jesus Christ is there, the world will come up to Jerusalem, and many nations will be converted. Notice it mentions "Philistia, and Tyre, with Ethiopia." This is all tremendously interesting when we remember that as the gospel left the land of Israel and started down the highways of the world, the first convert was the Ethiopian eunuch (Acts 8). He was born again out there in the desert. But the psalmist here has reference to, I believe, the entire nation of Ethiopia, which will be converted in that future time.

And of Zion it shall be said, This and that man was born in her: and the highest himself shall establish her [Ps. 87:5].

The King of Kings will make Zion the capital of the earth.

The Lord shall count, when he writeth up the people, that this man was born there. Selah [Ps. 87:6].

There will be many who will turn to the Lord in that day, recognizing that they were deceived by the Antichrist. What a glorious time this will be!

PSALM 88

THEME: Confidence in God in the midst of suffering

This is "A Song or Psalm for the sons of Korah, to the chief Musician upon Mahalath Leannoth, Maschil of Heman the Ezrahite." It is a doleful psalm. Psalm 87 was all glory; this psalm is all gloom. It is a lamentation. It is the darkest wail of woe in the Book of Psalms.

> **O Lord God of my salvation, I have cried day and night before thee [Ps. 88:1].**

The one ray of hope in this psalm is that He is the "God of my salvation," and the psalmist is holding on to that. It is mere speculation, of course, but this psalm has been applied to Job and to Uzziah who had leprosy and to Jeremiah in the dungeon and to Hezekiah when he was sick. But no matter who is in view, this psalm describes great suffering. Yet in all of his suffering and affliction he maintains his confidence in God as the God of his salvation. That is the great theme of this psalm.

> **I am afflicted and ready to die from my youth up: while I suffer thy terrors I am distracted [Ps. 88:15].**

He is in a tough place. Wrath, death, the grave, and darkness are summed up together by the sufferer.

> **Thy fierce wrath goeth over me; thy terrors have cut me off.**
>
> **They came round about me daily like water; they compassed me about together.**
>
> **Lover and friend hast thou put far from me, and mine acquaintance into darkness [Ps. 88:16–18].**

Unlike other psalms which begin with deep distress but end with the joy of deliverance, this psalm closes with the word *darkness*. Hengstenberg has this comment: "The Psalm ends with an energetic expression of its main thought—the immediate vicinity of death. The darkness is thickest at the end just as it is in the morning, before the rising of the sun."

PSALM 89

THEME: Psalm of the Davidic covenant

This is the final psalm in the Leviticus section. *The New Scofield Reference Bible* calls it the psalm of the Davidic Covenant. I like that because it is what the psalm is all about. This great psalm was written by Ethan the Ezrahite. It is a maschil, which means it is one of instruction. Ethan was probably a singer who belonged to the tribe of Levi. The writer is not identified for us—purposely, I think—because it is the faithfulness of God that is exalted in this psalm. The faithfulness of God is mentioned ten times, which makes it obvious that the psalmist is emphasizing His faithfulness. The word *covenant* is mentioned four times, and with it God says, "I have sworn" three times. Also "I will not lie" occurs four times. It is quite a contrast to the previous psalm which was all gloom and no glory. This one is all glory and no gloom. It is a psalm of great excitement, and it rests upon the covenant that God made with David. When we were studying 2 Samuel, we spent quite a bit of time in chapter 7 which records God's covenant with David. If you want to know how important it is, you will find it referred to again and again in the writings of the prophets, and here is a psalm devoted to it.

> **I will sing of the mercies of the LORD for ever: with my mouth will I make known thy faithfulness to all generations [Ps. 89:1].**

Is God good to you? I am sure He is. He certainly is good to me, and because of that "I will sing of the mercies of the LORD for ever." Although I can't really sing, I am going to tell it out the best way I know how. The mercies of the Lord are wonderful!

"With my mouth will I make known thy faithfulness"—I'm glad he didn't say "sing" this time, because singing excludes me; but I can use my mouth to make known His faithfulness. My, how faithful He has been to me!

Notice the pronoun is "thy"—it is *God's* faithfulness. It is praise to God for His faithfulness to David. Then down in verse 24 we read, "But my faithfulness and my mercy shall be with him." The pronoun has changed because it is God speaking. All the references in this psalm, regardless of the pronoun used, refer to the faithfulness of God.

For I have said, Mercy shall be built up for ever: thy faithfulness shalt thou establish in the very heavens [Ps. 89:2].

God is faithful. Our salvation rests upon the death of Christ and the faithfulness of God in saving those who put their trust in Him. It is what *God says* that is important.

It reminds me of the little Scottish lady I have told you about. She had sent her boy away to school, and he had come home a skeptic. She was fixing breakfast for him one morning and telling him how God had saved her, how sure she was of it, and how wonderful His salvation was. Finally the son could stand it no longer. He blurted out, "Your little soul doesn't amount to anything! It is very small compared to this great universe. God could forget you and wouldn't even miss you." On and on he talked. Then there was silence. This little Scottish mother kept quiet for a while. She finished serving him breakfast and sat down to eat. Then she said, "Son, I have been thinking about it. Maybe you are right. It may be that my soul doesn't amount to anything, but if I lose my soul, God is going to lose more than I will lose." Her son asked, "What do you mean by that?" Her reply was this, "If I lose my soul—you've just said it doesn't amount to much—so I wouldn't lose much, but God would lose a great deal. He would lose His Word, His reputation, because He *said* He would save me!"

She was right. And God would lose His reputation if He did not make good His covenant to David. But God is faithful.

> **I have made a covenant with my chosen, I have sworn
> unto David my servant [Ps. 89:3].**

God says He made a covenant with David.

> **And the heavens shall praise thy wonders, O LORD: thy
> faithfulness also in the congregation of the saints [Ps.
> 89:5].**

"The heavens declare the glory of God; and the firmament sheweth his handiwork" (Ps. 19:1), but the faithfulness of God has more glory connected with it than that. "O LORD: thy faithfulness also in the congregation of the saints." His faithfulness toward us deserves our praise!

> **O LORD God of hosts, who is a strong LORD like unto
> thee? or to thy faithfulness round about thee? [Ps. 89:8].**

We certainly get the impression that he is talking about the faithfulness of God.

> **I have found David my servant; with my holy oil have I
> anointed him [Ps. 89:20].**

God says, "I will make good what I promised David at the time I anointed him."

God rests upon what He has promised David:

> **But my faithfulness and my mercy shall be with him:
> and in my name shall his horn be exalted [Ps. 89:24].**

The "horn" speaks of his strength.

> **Also I will make him my firstborn, higher than the
> kings of the earth [Ps. 89:27].**

God's covenant to David was that He would be sending One in his line. The covenant centers on the Lord Jesus Christ. Of Him God says,

"Also I will make him my firstborn, higher than the kings of the earth." Look at this—it is wonderful. When God sent the Lord Jesus into this world, He came as the only begotten Son, and by His incarnation yonder at Bethlehem He became the Son of God. Thus He was revealed in His life of humiliation—God manifested in the flesh. And after He died a sacrificial death—for that is the reason He came from heaven—He became in resurrection the firstborn, the first begotten from the dead. He is speaking of the resurrected Christ: "Also I will make him my firstborn"—the resurrected Christ, the One who came back from the dead after He had died on the cross. It simply means that the scepter of this universe is in nail pierced hands.

But we are told here that He is "higher than the kings of the earth." This means that He is Lord of Lords and King of Kings! The psalmist now is talking about the Lord Jesus. Therefore again He says:

> My mercy will I keep for him for evermore, and my covenant shall stand fast with him [Ps. 89:28].

Now we must correctly divide the Word of Truth. Verses 29–32 cannot speak of Christ, but of David's posterity. Suppose that David's children forsake God. What will God do?

> If his children forsake my law, and walk not in my judgments;
>
> If they break my statutes, and keep not my commandments;
>
> Then will I visit their transgression with the rod, and their iniquity with stripes [Ps. 89:30–32].

Does it sound as though God is through with His children if they are not faithful to Him? No!

> Nevertheless my lovingkindness will I not utterly take from him, nor suffer my faithfulness to fail [Ps. 89:33].

Oh, my friend, I may be faithless; but my God is *faithful*. What wonderful assurance!

Next God takes an oath concerning the covenant He made with David:

> **My covenant will I not break, nor alter the thing that is gone out of my lips.**
>
> **Once have I sworn by my holiness that I will not lie unto David.**
>
> **His seed shall endure for ever, and his throne as the sun before me [Ps. 89:34-36].**

At this very moment there is One sitting at the right hand of God who is coming to earth to sit on that throne of David. He is the Lord Jesus Christ, the Son of David.

> **It shall be established for ever as the moon, and as a faithful witness in heaven. Selah [Ps. 89:37].**

David will have a Son who will sit on the throne of this universe. That fact is as established as the moon is established in the heavens, and it looks like the moon is going to be there for a long time. God will make good His covenant with David.

> **Lord, where are thy former lovingkindnesses, which thou swarest unto David in thy truth? [Ps. 89:49].**

To these people who had gotten away from God at this time, it looked as if God had forgotten His covenant. But He hadn't forgotten His covenant. God is faithful. God has the Man to sit on David's throne.

BIBLIOGRAPHY
(Recommended for Further Study)

Alexander, J. A. *The Psalms*. 1864. Reprint. Grand Rapids, Michigan: Zondervan Publishing House, 1964.

Gaebelein, Arno C. *The Annotated Bible*. 1917. Reprint. Neptune, New Jersey: Loizeaux Brothers, 1970.

Gaebelein, Arno C. *The Book of Psalms*. 1939. Reprint. Neptune, New Jersey: Loizeaux Brothers, 1965. (The finest prophetical interpretation of the Psalms)

Grant, F. W. *The Psalms*. Neptune, New Jersey: Loizeaux Brothers, 1895. (Numerical Bible)

Gray, James M. *Synthetic Bible Studies*. Old Tappan, New Jersey: Fleming H. Revell Co., 1906.

Ironside, H. A. *The Psalms*. Neptune, New Jersey: Loizeaux Brothers, n.d.

Jamieson, Robert; Fausset, A. R.; and Brown, D. *Commentary on the Bible*. 3 vols. Grand Rapids, Michigan: Wm. B. Eerdmans Publishing Co., 1945.

Jensen, Irving L. *The Psalms*. Chicago, Illinois: Moody Press, 1970. (A self-study guide)

Morgan, G. Campbell. *Notes on the Psalms*. Old Tappan, New Jersey: Fleming H. Revell Co., 1947.

Olson, Erling C. *Meditations in the Psalms*. Neptune, New Jersey: Loizeaux Brothers, 1939. (Devotional)

Perowne, J. J. Stewart. *The Book of Psalms*. 1882. Reprint. Grand Rapids, Michigan: Zondervan Publishing House, 1976.

Sauer, Erich. *The Dawn of World Redemption*. Grand Rapids, Michigan: Wm. B. Eerdmans Publishing Co., 1951. (An excellent Old Testament survey)

Scroggie, W. Graham. *The Psalms*. Old Tappan, New Jersey: Fleming H. Revell Co., 1948. (Excellent)

Scroggie, W. Graham. *The Unfolding Drama of Redemption*. Grand Rapids, Michigan: Zondervan Publishing House, 1970. (An excellent survey and outline of the Old Testament)

Spurgeon, Charles Haddon. *The Treasury of David*. 3 vols. Reprint. Grand Rapids, Michigan: Zondervan Publishing House, 1974. (A classic work and very comprehensive)

Unger, Merrill F. *Unger's Bible Handbook*. Chicago, Illinois: Moody Press, 1966. (A basic tool for every Christian's library)

Unger, Merrill F. *Unger's Commentary on the Old Testament*. Vol. 1. Chicago, Illinois: Moody Press, 1981. (A fine summary of each paragraph; Highly recommended)